Wax on Crafts Holiday Projects

Wax on Crafts
Holiday Projects

Miriam Joy

Schiffer Publishing Ltd

4880 Lower Valley Road • Atglen, PA 19310

Other Schiffer Books by the Author:
Miriam Joy's Wax Design Techniques
ISBN: 978-0-7643-4467-1

Other Schiffer Books on Related Subjects:
Decorating Eggs: Exquisite Designs with Wax & Dye
ISBN: 978-0-7643-4654-5

Designed by RoS
Type set in Blueprint MT/Candara

ISBN: 978-0-7643-4955-3
Printed in China

Published by Schiffer Publishing, Ltd.
4880 Lower Valley Road
Atglen, PA 19310
Phone: (610) 593-1777; Fax: (610) 593-2002
E-mail: Info@schifferbooks.com

For our complete selection of fine books on this and related subjects, please visit our website at www.schifferbooks.com. You may also write for a free catalog.

This book may be purchased from the publisher. Please try your bookstore first.

We are always looking for people to write books on new and related subjects. If you have an idea for a book, please contact us at proposals@schifferbooks.com.

Schiffer Publishing's titles are available at special discounts for bulk purchases for sales promotions wor premiums. Special editions, including personalized covers, corporate imprints, and excerpts can be created in large quantities for special needs. For more information, contact the publisher.

Dedication

To my daughter Cheyenne,
whom I love with my whole
heart. You were always my little
shadow. I think you started doing
arts and crafts with me from the time
you could hold a crayon. If I created
something, you created with me. You
spent a lot of your little life with me at the
tole painting store where I taught. You had
your own little painted stool that you would sit
on. I do not believe there was a time that you did
not love art. Soon after you started "topping" me in
every project we did. You have a God-given talent. If I
wanted to know if the color was right or if something was
placed right, I would ask you. You were around five or six at
this time.

I knew you were special when we happened to see a sunset—not
a brightly colored one, just a sunset with very little color. You looked
up and said, "I see blue, I see white, I see gray, I see green, I see pink, I
see orange, I see yellow, I see purple." I had to look again, this time really
look. You got it. You can see colors that the ordinary person does not, or does
not take the time to see. You saw all the colors in the box of crayons. Each color
spoke to you.

Thank you for loving the holidays as much as I do, for helping me decorate and making
each one special. The baking we did just so we could decorate the cookies or cakes to
make them pretty. All the trips to the pumpkin patch. You loved pumpkins and you had a
collection of real pumpkins every year. I will never look at a "plumpkin" without seeing you.

You have brought such joy to my life. I saw you blossom in art. The proudest moment of my life was
when you stopped listening to everyone else and followed your heart. I could not be a prouder parent
than when you received your degree in art. You are an amazing artist and more so, a caring and loving
person. I know you will find your niche and conquer the world and make it a more colorful place.

Keep believing in yourself. Believe in your talents and create your own path. No matter what, I will be proud of
you. The most important title I can realize is to be Cheyenne's Mom.

Acknowledgments

I cannot start a book without first acknowledging the Lord Jesus Christ and all the ways He has blessed me. It is because of His love and blessings that any of this is possible. I thank Him for allowing me to shine His light in my little corner of the art world, and for bestowing on me the gift of art that has so richly blessed my life.

To the most wonderful husband in the world, I could not be Miriam Joy without my Buddy Boy. How can I begin to express my love and appreciation for all you do? You are the support crew that keeps me going. I struggle to find the words to express all that you do for me, both as an artist and businesswoman, but most importantly as my partner. You make me feel like the most loved woman in the world. I love our long walks and our heartwarming talks. Sitting with you in the swing with your arms around me and falling asleep at night in your arms. Thank you for being my husband and my best friend. I love you so much.

It takes a village to run Miriamjoy.com and, trust me, I could not do it without my village. From the people who believed in us and do our manufacturing to our very special friends who help out with products, you are wonderful people. Thank you for all you have done. For all the people who have helped us along the way, friends and family who have prayed for my business, special people who helped edit my books—you guys are the best village a girl could have.

To our children: each one of you has helped in your own special way. You believed in me and have helped me out so much. I cannot thank you enough for your love and support.

··· Testimonial ···

I met Miriam Joy about four years ago and she and Bud have changed my life greatly. She had a smile on her face and greeted me like we have known each other for many years. I had the opportunity to take a Miriam Joy class and boy was that fun! Miriam Joy is a great teacher.

Once you have met Miriam Joy, you will not forget her. Not only does she love to share her art with others, but also her love of her Lord Jesus Christ. To know her is to love her. Where she finds the time to develop new tools, make new designs, make videos, teach, and write books, we'll never know. I know of a time or two when she was up for days with a design on her mind and couldn't sleep until she had it down on paper, rock, gourd, or whatever. I'm exhausted just thinking of it. If you have met Miriam Joy and Bud, you have met two of the most wonderful people in the world. Miriam Joy makes no bones about the loves of her life, The Lord, Bud, her family, and her art. You will never forget her—this I can promise you.

Thank You for all that you have shared with me and others, your love of Jesus, your friendship, your art and your faith in me.

—Doris Trombley
Gourd artist and teacher

Add a little "Joy" to your life!

Contents

Introduction

Who would have thought there are so many bright and wonderful designs that you could add to items with a box of crayons. A box of crayons! Never in my wildest dreams would I have believed that I would be making my living using crayons. People ask me what I do for a living and I tell them, "I play with crayons." They look to see if someone is there to take me away to the funny farm. Fun farm is right! I have so much fun in my studio, thinking of all the items that I can turn into extraordinary items, items that you may never give a second look or think about decorating. The first thing I applied the crayon wax to was gourds, but as any artist or crafter knows, you are always looking for the next thing to use as a canvas. Now, hundreds of wax-design projects later, I am stilled amazed at how adding wax to an item can create such a stunning and wonderful piece. Add that to a love for the holidays, decorating, and making wonderful gifts for all the people on your list.

My newest love is Twice-Melted Wax: a process of applying the wax and melting it again. You can create such wonderful things—from Christmas ornaments to Easter eggs, necklaces, and picture frames. I have just begun to explore all of the bright and colorful projects that I can create using this method.

My goal is to get you thinking outside the box and of all the different things you can add wax to. So let's get started and brighten up some of those old family treasures. Add a little color to the old basket grandma has sitting in the corner. Make a wonderful Christmas heirloom out of the old family sled. Add a harvest design to Uncle Joe's old saw that will be the talk ofthe Thanksgiving table.

··· Warnings and Precautions ···

As with any crafting project, it's important to understand the warnings and precautions as you move through the steps of colorful creation. Note the following:

1. MJ Low Temp Melting Pot, MJ Wax Design Tools, Embossing Tool, and the MJ Texture Brush Insert can all get very HOT. Use caution and do not touch the hot metal when using or handling these items. Be careful touching items heated with these tools. **They can become very HOT.**

2. Always have adult supervision in cases where children are using the wax design process. Safety allows fun for everyone! Wax design is not recommended for children under eight years of age.

3. The MJ Melting pot is an electrical device—caution should be used while using any electrical device.

4. Use caution when working with a hobby knife: if a tool can cut through a crayon, it can cut you, too!

5. Unplug the melting pot when not in use. **Do not leave the melting pot unattended!**

Author Note

It does not take a lot of money to make wonderful items, just a little imagination. For example, those wonderful boxes you get special surprises in or that heart-shaped box of wonderfully delicious chocolates. Turn them into a treat for a second time.

A lot of my craft adventures start with a trip to my local thrift store, or—my personal favorite—a dollar store (there are many franchises under varied names all selling things for one dollar). There I find seasonal items that *scream* to be decorated in wax: heart bottles, glass items of all shapes and sizes, foam pumpkins, glitter decorations, and glass candle stands.

Glass candle stands and glass vases are among my most-loved craft items. You can use them in so many ways. You can even add height to an item or just "class it up." Candles are another favorite from the dollar stores, especially for the holidays. Everyone loves them and they are a wonderful gift for all the people on your list. You can use colored or plain candles. There are also the tapered candles that usually come two to a box.

The thrift store is great for baskets. You can usually find all shapes and sizes there. Look for other items to apply wax to— like an old saw, sled, or something else that attracts your eye. I find some of my picture frames and stamps in the dollar section of the craft store. I look for big clearance sales after the holidays when items are marked eighty to ninety percent off. During that time, I pick up my glass ornaments and seasonal ribbon.

I am always saying: "It is amazing what you can make with inexpensive or dollar items and a little wax."

Note: Read through the varied project instructions I've included for you here in their entirety before beginning. Then, if there is a video, though you do not need to view it to work on or complete your project, sometimes it's fun to see the design come together before digging in! Have fun!

Using Crayola Crayons as Wax

For my wax I use Crayola crayons. Don't you love Crayola crayons? The smell brings back wonderful memories to the old and young alike. But seriously, where else can you find all of these colors in one box? And when you start to mix and match all the colors, it becomes unlimited.

Other waxes can be thin and require you to add color, so why not use crayons? It does make a difference for you to use Crayola brand crayons, though. They are brighter, thicker, and the color does not fade. At back-to-school time, you cannot beat the price of a box of twenty-four crayons—my favorite box. It has all the basic colors that I use the most and, as I said, is very cost-effective.

One of the things people are most amazed by is that each color works a little differently. The lighter colors, like yellow and yellow-greens, are thinner in consistency. It is not that you are doing anything wrong as you melt the crayon. The darker colors are a little thicker. Of course, there is one in every bunch that has to make its own rules, and for the Crayola crayons, it

is white. The white crayon thinks it is a thicker color and goes on thicker, but can also act like a thinner color and can drip a little more.

When you are working with crayons, the tip of the crayon is the color the wax is going to be. Do not expect your color to come out the color of the label surrounding the crayon. A lot of the darker colors, such as blue or purple, look black when applied as wax. Make the color lighter by adding a sliver of white, until you get the desired color.

Treat your crayons just like paints. Mix and match them in the same way. For example, blue, green, and white mixed in equal amounts makes a beautiful turquoise color.

Of course the bigger boxes of crayons have a bigger variety of colors. You start to see gold, silver, bronze, and copper crayons. Just keep in mind that if you are doing a bigger project, you may need a couple crayons of the same color. (Colors like inchworm and mac and cheese are among my favorites.) The Crayola Gel FX crayons have bright and vivid colors.

There are boxes of metallic and glitter crayons available, too. The metallic crayons have that metallic shine and can add so much to designs or Christmas ornaments. The glitter crayons contain glitter to give projects that extra sparkle. Just remember when using these colors, they add the sparkle and shine, but not the brightness that the regular crayons bring.

Do not be afraid to use old crayons. They do not go bad. Broken, worn, or discarded, they still work great. The end of a school year when kids are throwing away the worn-down or broken crayons and Sunday school programs can be among some of the best places to get unwanted crayons. Also, white is not a favorite color, so it may be easy to come by!

··· About MJ Wax Tools ···

The Miriam Joy Product line was created by dreaming. I started playing with wax and realized how amazing it was. I knew that there were so many ways to use it, but I needed tools that I could not find at the craft store. I found that I also wanted to teach other people this wonderful process and to share my love for wax with them. But they, too, needed to be able to get the tools to create beautiful and fun pieces. So I began to create them, one at a time—there were a few fail-and-expensive attempts, but the Miriam Joy tool line began to emerge. The first one was a customized melting pot, followed by the wax tools. Then, to go along with the products, I began to provide YouTube videos for fun projects to help and inspire crafters everywhere. (See **www.youtube.com/user/Miriamjoy123**).

As I continue to find new ways to use the wax, I continue to make new tools. I hope to keep growing the tool line. To order Miriam Joy Products please visit me at www.MiriamJoy.com.

Note: *I try to keep all the customized MJ Products made in the United States were we can also help other artists and companies grow. We have had a lot of people help us along the way, so it is important for Miriam Joy to help others.*

MJ Low Temp Melting Pot

Use an MJ Low Temp Melting Pot to melt the crayons. The melting pot is UL rated and is 120°F, the perfect temperature to melt crayons without getting the wax too hot. Keeping the wax confined to the little well is what allows you to use such a small amount of crayon. The well provides an area for you to dip your wax tool. Most melting pots are round or other shapes. It would take around twenty crayons to fill up other melting pots because they do not have a well, which is what makes this process work. I have tried several other items and methods to melt my wax and have had no success when using the tools. The MJ Melting Pot is customized to keep your tool in the well.

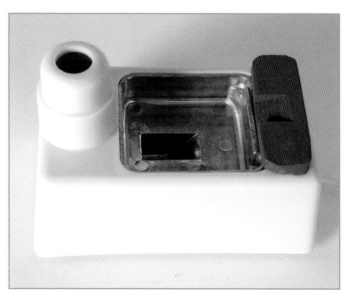

MJ Wax Design Tools

I have designed a line of MJ Wax Tools and have had them manufactured just for this process. They each have a foam handle to keep them from getting warm while being held. The foam handle also makes them comfortable to hold. The tools are well-balanced. There are four MJ Wax Design Tools. Each tool has two different sized tips, so that it is like getting two tools in each one, and who doesn't love a two for one deal?

The type of metal for these tools does matter. Aluminum tools will not work with this process, as aluminum does not hold the heat evenly and the wax does not stick to the tool. Wooden-handle tools do not hold the heat as well, and the wood handle gets very warm. After heating and cooling the wood handle tools, the tips tend to come unglued from the wood. On the MJ tool, the balls on each end hold the wax on the tool. A lot of thought and trial and error went into designing these tools. I have found that people who have had a hard time holding other tools, due to arthritis and other medical conditions, find these tools easier to use.

MJ Wax Design Tool #2 is the tool I designed first, and is still the tool I use the most and the first tool that I start my students with. If you can only start with one tool, this is the one I recommend.

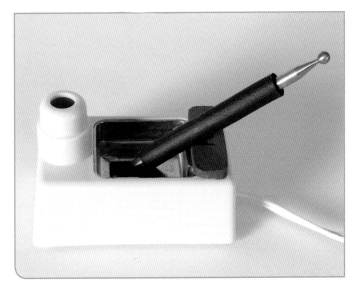

MJ Wax Design Tool setting in melting pot

- MJ Wax Design Tool #2 is ³⁄₁₆" on one end and ¼" on the other end. Tools bigger than this size drip a little too much.

- MJ Wax Design Tool #1 is a step down from the #2 tool. If you want a medium-sized stroke, this is a tool for you. MJ Wax Design Tool #1 is ⅛" on one end and ⁵⁄₃₂" on the other end.

- MJ Wax Design Tool #0 is a smaller tool and used for smaller work. It creates smaller strokes. MJ Wax Design Tool #0 is ²⁄₂₅" on one end and ¹⁄₁₀" on the other end.

- MJ Wax Design Tool #00 is the smallest of the tools. This tool is designed for fine detail work or where other strokes cannot fit. The size of the tool is ³⁄₆₄" on one end and .072 inches on the other end.

The size of the tool you use determines the size of the stroke or dot. If you need a larger, longer stroke or dot, use a bigger tool. If you need a little or short stroke or dot, use a smaller tool. If you need fine tiny details, use the MJ Wax Design Tool #00.

MJ Texture Brush and Insert

The MJ Texture Brush and Insert is designed to create textured backgrounds: trees, bushes, and grass. It also makes wonderful snow.

Directions: The insert is placed on top of the MJ Melting Pot when the melting pot is empty. After the insert has warmed, melt the crayon on the insert. Use your MJ Texture Brush to apply the melting crayon onto your project.

While the MJ Texture Brush was designed for wax, it works great with paints as well.

I have made a video to help you with this process at:
http://youtu.be/1oORrPRGOBo

MJ Texture Brush and Insert

Sit the insert into the empty melting pot.

Allow the insert to warm.

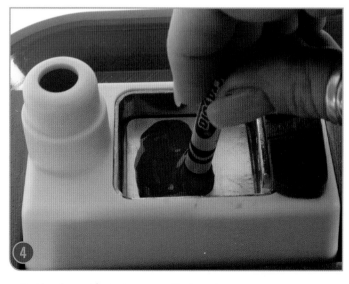

Apply a layer of crayon across the insert.

Pounce the MJ Texture Brush into the melted crayon.

13

MJ Wax Brushes

MJ Wax Brushes were designed to apply a layer of melted wax.

Directions: The brush is dipped into the well of the melting pot to pick up wax. This is one of the times that you can fill the melting pot above the well if you like. While the wax is still warm, apply it to your project. You can apply a second coat if needed. Let the first coat harden or cool and then reapply.

You do use more wax with this method. I do not clean these brushes. They are inexpensive enough to keep one for each color. I have also added foam to this brush to make it easier to handle and to keep it from getting warm. To straighten the bristles when using a brush with cold wax in the bristles, set the brush into the well of the melting pot to re-warm the wax.

There is a video to help you with this process at:
http://youtu.be/mp7rpBmRAS0

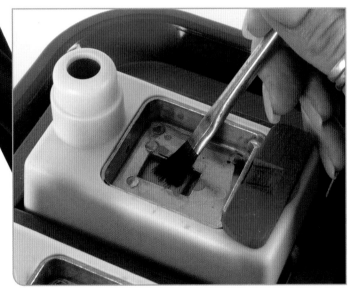

Load your MJ Wax Brush with wax from the melting pot well.

Glass Eyedroppers

There are times when the brushes and MJ Wax Tools are just not enough. The glass eyedropper applies the wax more thickly and can reach places you cannot. They are great for making thicker lines. This is one of the times that you can fill the melting pot above the well if you like.

Directions: Set the glass eyedropper into the well with the melting crayon and let it warm. It is important that you use a *glass* eyedropper. Plastic ones will melt. Push in the rubber bulb to bring the melted crayon into the tube. Then apply wax onto your project.

This is another item that is inexpensive enough that you can keep one for each color. You *can* clean them out, but it takes time. Make sure when you are done with the glass eyedropper that you squeeze the bulb and get all of the wax out. You do not want the wax to dry up in the bulb. This causes the bulb to harden; then you cannot squeeze melted wax up or out the glass tube.

There is a video to help you with this process at:
http://youtu.be/cv5MiEg4-wc

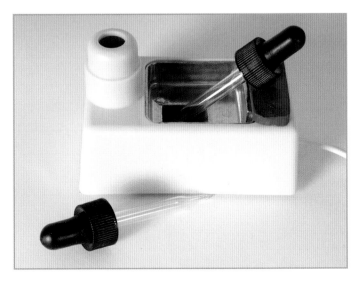

MJ Three Pot Tray

I've designed a tray that holds the melting pots in place. This makes the melting pots more secure and less likely to move. I suggest you place the electrical cords going away from you so that you do not get tangled up in them. Then hook them up to a single power cord with multiple outlets and an on/off switch on the cord so you can turn them on and off with ease at the same time. The red light on the power strip also lets you know if the melting pots are still on.

The tray has a lip to help keep everything contained. The tray helps keep the wax off you. If the wax is going to drip, it will most likely drip here. By the way, I recommend working in an old shirt or an apron since crayon is hard to get out of your clothes.

There is a video to help you with this process at:
http://youtu.be/6oIoXDV-Iq8

MJ Dry Board

The MJ Dry Board has little plastic spikes so that you can continue to dry your project after you have colored or varnished it without the project sticking to the board.

Directions: You should not spray varnish on the MJ Dry Board. Varnish the project first and then place it onto the board to continue drying.

There is a video to help you with this process at:
http://youtu.be/Mu9uv_dtJoA

Load wax into an MJ Wax Liner.

MJ Wax Liner

The wax liner is used for those times when you really need to make a straight line. You can write with it, make very small dots, or use it to outline your artwork to make it look fresh. It makes great pine needles for trees.

Directions: Place the wax liner into the melting pot well with melted wax; allow it to warm for forty-five seconds to a minute. Once warm, scoop up the wax and tool and you are ready to begin your project. As long as you warmed your tool long enough,

you will be able to write for quite a while before it stops. When the wax runs out, or the wax cools, set the wax liner back into the well to re-warm. To clean the tool, dump all of the wax out. Wipe the outside with a paper towel. Take a Q-tip and push it into the well of the wax liner to remove any remaining wax.

There is a video to help you with this process at:
http://youtu.be/5GcYQNMhdAo

MJ Craft Templates

MJ Craft Templates were invented first, out of my frustration at not being able to create the perfect shape; and second, out of my desire to find a better way to create designs or trace more exacting patterns. While other templates are made of plastic or paper and are contained all on one sheet, the MJ Craft Templates are made of flexible rubber and can be used on round or square objects. They are the first templates that can go around the corner of a wall. These templates are great for many crafting needs, such as school projects, quilting, woodworking, stained-glass work and gourding—just to name a few. The MJ Craft Templates are made of $\frac{1}{16}$"-rubber and come in a variety of shapes and sizes. The rubber allows the templates to hold in place without slipping while tracing the shape.

There is a video to show you how to use the craft templates at:
http://youtu.be/nc09fhVwBbY

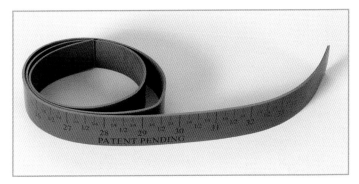

There is also a rubber ruler, called an MJ Flex-e, that is great for measuring projects. The rubber helps hold the ruler in place so you can measure items with ease. Just place the Flex-e around the project and put a little tension on the ruler and it will hold in place while you measure.

There is a video to show you how to use the Flex-e at:
http://youtu.be/xEhY2j-zm7M

Basic Supplies

Removable Glue Dots

Removable glue dots are used when you need a little help holding the craft template in place or if the templates are larger than you can easily hold with one hand while marking. I cut the glue dots in half to fit the craft template, thus making the package of glue dots go twice as far.

Directions: Apply glue dots to at least four places on the template. Place the template on your project and trace your shape. Remove the template and pull off the glue dots. It is important to use removable glue dots: they are designed with removal in mind.

QuikWood®

QuikWood is a great two-part epoxy created to fix any wood project that needs fixing. However, I use it as a sculpting medium like clay. It has a workable time of thirty minutes and is rock-hard in an hour. The short dry time makes it great for fast, fun art projects.

White Charcoal Pencil

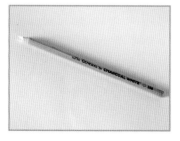

To trace the shapes onto a project, I use a white charcoal pencil. It leaves a bright enough line to see easily and can be removed. Unlike some craft pencils, you can put the charcoal pencil in a pencil sharpener to sharpen it.

Directions: If the pencil is not leaving a dark enough line, simply take the pencil and use a flame from a cigarette lighter, or other type of flame, to warm the pencil tip. This makes that pencil line bright and removes any wax buildup that you may have on the pencil.

Hobby Knife with Shovel Blade

I use a hobby knife with a shovel nose blade to remove unwanted wax. It allows you to maneuver in between your strokes when removing crayon, so that if you make a mistake or if you have an unwanted drop of wax, you can simply remove it.

Directions: Always use your hobby knife at an angle when removing wax. Holding the knife with the blade straight up and down causes scratching to occur. Start at the biggest end of the stroke or drop and work toward the small end. This allows you to get under the wax more easily and you can remove more of the wax this way.

Mr. Clean Magic Eraser

I have found that a Mr. Clean Magic Eraser makes removing the charcoal pencil lines easy. They can be found in the bathroom cleaning supply section at most stores. I cut my sponge into three sections; it is a bit easier to use this way and lasts a little longer.

Directions: Wet it slightly and wring out all the water. Wipe the area that shows the charcoal pencil. This will leave a chalky white film behind. Lightly dampen a paper towel and remove the film.

There is a video to help you with this process at:
http://youtu.be/voGnUzpENYl

Embossing Tool

The embossing tool is also called a heat gun, and can be found in the scrapbook section of the craft stores. Use the embossing tool to reheat the wax in a method I call twice melted, or for heat setting any base coat that uses inks or dyes.

Cleanup Supplies

Of course, the most important items are the cleanup supplies. These make cleaning a breeze. Cotton balls are used to absorb the crayon and clean the MJ Melting Pot. Cotton swabs are used to clean the MJ Wax Liner. Damp Q-tips can also be used to remove charcoal pencil lines in hard-to-get-to areas. Paper towels are used to wipe and clean your MJ Wax Design Tools as well as to clean the MJ Texture Brush and Insert.

Acrylic Paints

I work with acrylic paints the most and base-coat a lot of my projects with them. I love to work with acrylic paints; they are easy to use, dry fast, and are water-based for an easy cleanup.

Directions: You may need to base-coat a few layers of paint to get the paint even. You can also add a little water to your paint and apply a wash. This makes a nice thinner layer of paint.

Varnish, Glaze, Lacquer, and Epoxy Resin

For the wax process, I use different finishes for different projects, depending on how much the project is going to be handled, or if the project is flat or whether it will be exposed to the sun.

Spray-on varnish works great, but a lot of people are intimidated by sprays. Do not let spray varnishes worry you—just try it. Practice until you get comfortable. Runs can be caused by getting too close or going too slowly when varnishing. Varnish in a ventilated area. If you are working outside

in the sun, remember that you are working with wax and you cannot leave it in the sun to dry.

Directions: Start by shaking your can to mix the varnish. Spray about twelve inches away from your project. Start on one side of your project, working in a back-and-forth motion. Do not use a circular motion. It does not cover evenly. Place your project on the MJ Dry Board so that it can continue to dry without sticking to the project. Once the varnish dries to the touch, apply another coat. Applying varnish not only protects the wax, but also brings out the color of the wax (crayon). Apply at least two to three coats.

The humidity can cause your varnish to turn white. That is why I like to use gloss. It is less likely to turn white. If your varnish should turn white, let it dry and varnish it again on a dryer day to turn it back to its original state.

You can use brush-on varnish if you have used acrylic paint or have heat set your dyes so they will not run. Brush-on varnish can pick up the dye or color and bring it over your wax, so make sure that, when using it, your color has been heat set before you apply your wax design. Brush-on varnishes are usually thicker and result in better coverage.

I use glazes and lacquer on glass projects. It seems to go on well and does not show too much. I also use it over jewelry pieces to keep them from melting in the sun. The surface needs to be flat, and a thick layer of the glaze or lacquer needs to be applied. All of the wax must be covered. This sometimes can take more than one coat. Apply it by starting on the outside and working your way toward the middle. You can also apply it by putting it into a bowl and brushing it on.

Epoxy resin is heat- and waterproof. You need to be able to apply it to a flat project. This will protect the wax and keep it from melting. The epoxy resin consists of two parts and you need to follow the manufacturer's instructions. It will give you a very thick and glossy finish. Do not apply epoxy resin over twice-melted wax where the project is solid wax. The resin does not have anything to adhere to and it will peel off the wax.

Setting Up Your Tray

1.

Place your MJ Low Temp Melting Pots into the tray.

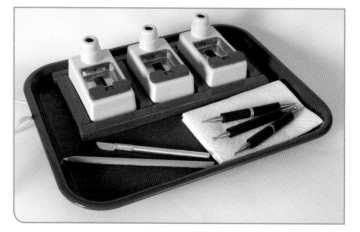

Place the cords away from you to keep yourself from getting tangled in them. I use a power strip to keep the melting pots plugged into, so that I do not have to unplug all of the melting pots individually. I can just flip the switch and turn them off and on. If you have a red light on the power stripd, it helps to keep track whether they are off or on.

Fold your paper towel into fours. Place it in the right-hand bottom corner and place your tools on top.

To the left of the bottom tray, keep the craft knife and white charcoal pencil so they will always be handy.

2.

Next, plug in your MJ Low Temp Melting Pot and get it warmed up. This only takes a few minutes, and you can load your crayon while it is still warming. Remember to use only Crayola brand crayons. (I will refer to Crayola crayons as wax, which is what they are.)

Holding the crayon with the tip pointed up, cut the crayon paper just above the word "Crayola."

3.

With your hobby knife, cut the paper down the side of the crayon to where you first cut the paper. Do not try to peel the paper back with the knife. It is much harder that way and you are more likely to cut yourself.

4.

Peel the paper off the crayon to where you cut it with the hobby knife. I leave the rest of the paper on my crayon. This keeps it clean and keeps from getting other colors on the crayon. I also leave the name of the crayon as the last part so that if I need to know what color it is, I have that information.

5.

Take your scissors and cut the crayon just above where you cut the paper.

6.

Cut that piece in half with your scissors. By breaking the crayon into two pieces, they fit into the well of the melting pot. It keeps the crayon from melting on the top layer of the well and wasting your wax.

7.

Put both pieces into the well. It is okay to get some of the crayon on the next level of the well—it just helps to keep it cleaner and avoids waste.

There is a video you can watch to show you how to cut and add the crayon at:
http://youtu.be/64wt_GAWB3s

Your melted crayon should not overflow into the second level.

8.

Your melted crayon should not overflow into the second level. You want to make sure that you do not fill the well too full unless you are working with the glass eyedropper or the MJ Wax Brushes. If the well is so full that you cannot see the rectangle of the well, you will start to drip more when working with the MJ Wax Tools. If you fill the well too full, simply take a cotton ball and absorb a little crayon.

> There is a video to help you know
> if you have too much crayon in the well at:
> **http://youtu.be/S6bcOZJoIZg**

9.

It is important to keep the well full. Do not let your well get less than three-quarters full. This helps keep your strokes the same size because you are picking up the same amount of wax. If you notice your strokes getting smaller, check the level of your wax.

10.

To add crayon to your well, take your scissors and cut the size of crayon piece you may need. I leave the paper on when I am doing this. A lot of times once it is cut, it comes out of the paper all by itself; if not, then cut the paper with your hobby knife and remove it.

> There is a video to help you know when to add
> more crayon to your well at:
> **http://youtu.be/LBQatFU1dnY**

Absorb just a little crayon with the cotton ball if the well is too full.

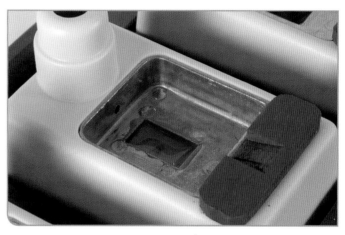

The right amount of wax in the well.

The level of wax when you need to add more crayon.

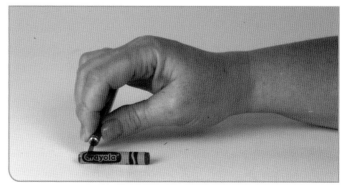

Keep the well full by adding more crayon as needed.

21

Loading Your Tool

1.

THIS IS THE MOST IMPORTANT INFORMATION TO MAKE THIS PROCESS WORK! If you do not warm your tools and try to apply warm wax with a cold tool, you will get a glob of wax. The wax will stick to the tool and not want to come off. It only takes about fifteen seconds or more to warm the tool. If the area you are working in is cooler, the tool may need a few seconds longer to warm.

2.

Make sure that the project you are working on is not cold. This will cause the wax not to work correctly. If your item is cold, allow it to warm up to room temperature. You can also warm it up with a blow dryer or embossing tool.

Start with the small end of the MJ Wax Design Tool #2. This is the easier of the tools to begin with.

3.

Place the tool into your wax and warm the end of your tool.

4.

Once your MJ Wax Design Tool is warm, place it in the deepest part of the well. Go all the way to the bottom. Touch the bottom and pull your tool straight out. By pulling it straight up, you get the maximum amount of wax. Do not pull the tool out slowly or come up along the side of the well. This removes some of the wax.

Watch yourself the first few times you load your strokes, as it is instinct to want to knock off the drip of wax. You want the drip. The drip is what adds texture to your stroke. You will not even know that you are doing this. Be careful not to form bad habits of stirring the drip, clicking the sides, or hitting it. The crayon should only be stirred if it has been sitting a while and the color has separated in the wax. White crayons need stirring a little more often, as do metallic and glitter crayons. The easiest way to do this is to not over-think it. Just go to the deepest part of the well, touch the bottom, and pull the tool straight out. Make sure that you load it in the same spot each time, as this will keep your strokes consistent in size.

5.

Know where you are going with your stroke before you pick it up. Do not load the wax and sit there and hold it while you are looking where to go. This cools your wax and your stroke will not go on smoothly. It is natural to get excited after putting on a stroke—while still holding the tool in your hand and allowing the tool to cool. Watch out for this. (I am the worst offender of holding the tool in my hand while talking to someone.) If you get distracted, just let the tool warm up again before your next stroke.

Warm your tools by placing them in the wax.

Place your tool in the deepest part of the well and pull straight up.

6.

Keep the project you are working on no farther than twelve inches from the melting pot. Any farther and your tool will start to cool off. If you notice a drip, see how far your project is from the melting pot. If drips continue, check to see if you are sitting in front of a breeze, like that from a fan, heater, or air conditioner.

There is a video to help you with this process at:
http://youtu.be/7TWjiINf3kQ

How to Make a Stroke

1.

Pick up a pencil and hold it in your hand as if you are going to write on something. See how you are holding the pencil sideways, while resting your hand on the paper. This is how you should hold the tool. By resting the side of your hand on your project surface, you gain control of the stroke. Do not try to hold your tool straight up and down or try to balance it with your little finger. Resting the heel of your hand will give you balance, you will have control over your stroke, and your lines will come out consistently straight. If you try to make the strokes with the tool straight up and down, without resting your hand on the surface, your strokes will wobble all over the place. Now pull the pencil toward you in a straight line.

2.

Start by practicing your strokes on a piece of paper. Load your tool with the wax: going to the deepest part of the well, touch the bottom and bring it straight out. Bring it to your paper. Make sure that you do not go too fast. This will cause the wax to drip. With your hand sideways, like you would hold a pencil, and your hand resting on the paper, pull the stroke toward you. Like brush work, you should pull your strokes directly toward you. Slowly set the tool on the paper, pulling it toward you until it runs out of wax. Most people lift the tool too early. Make sure you pull, pull, pull that stroke. You are starting with a bunch of wax and going until you run out of wax on the tool. Pulling the stroke until it runs out of wax results in a great tail on the stroke. Remember to always pull the stroke until it runs out or is stopped short by a pattern design.

There is a video to help you with this process at:
http://youtu.be/imRRnLwBdkw

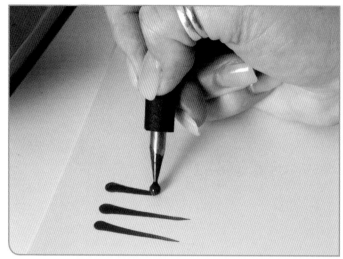

3.

Make sure that you are pulling your stroke nice and easy. Do not skim the top of the paper with the tool. Set the tool down and pull your stroke nice and slow. Pulling it too fast makes the wax skip. The slower you pull the stroke, the longer the stroke will become. If you notice that the edges of your strokes are uneven and are not smooth, you need to warm your tool a little more. Make sure when you are pulling your stroke that you do not twist the tool. This picks up wax from the back and makes the tail of the stroke uneven. Never go back over a stroke you do not like. The wax is already cooling and it will just make a mess.

There is a video to help you with this process at:
http://youtu.be/PH8tSEQYBJo

4.

Remember that the length and the width of the stroke are controlled by the size of the tool you use: the bigger the tool, the bigger the stroke; the smaller the tool, the smaller the stroke. You must reload for each stroke no matter how big or small the stroke is.

How to Make a Dot

Dots are loaded the same as a stroke. The size of the tool determines the size of the dot. Load the tool each time you make a dot. Do not think that you can load your tool anywhere in the well. Make sure that you go to the bottom of the well when loading the wax. This helps keep the dots consistent in size. You can also do a descending dot, which is a lot of fun. Load your tool and dot, dot, dot. Each successive dot will be smaller because you are running out of wax. I use this method a lot in my designs. You can do designs with just dots. You will also notice little tiny flecks of wax when you do the dots. The bigger the dot, the more flecks you get. If you are getting more than two flecks per dot, then slow down. You can remove them with your hobby knife or leave them depending on the texture of your design. Apply dots to areas that need cleaning up, like the ends of strokes or to help fill in an open area.

There is a video to help you with this process at:
http://youtu.be/7fGqF5YDpMI

Removing a Stroke, Dot, or Drop

Use a shovel tip on the hobby knife to remove a stroke, dot, or drop. The shovel tip lets you get in between your strokes and remove the wax you do not want. Allow the wax to harden or cool. Trying to remove wax while it is liquid is harder and can smear the color of the crayon, making a bigger mess to clean up.

1.

Put the hobby knife under the largest part of the stroke or dot. Starting with the largest part of the stroke will get a bigger piece of the wax off.

Always hold the hobby knife at an angle. Do not hold the knife straight up and down or scratches will occur. Turn the knife to the other angle to remove the tail part of the stroke.

2.

When you are removing the wax, you should not be able to hear any sound. If you hear scraping sounds, try a lighter touch.

If you need to remove any stain left behind from the wax, do so with a gum eraser. If you are going to put a stroke back on, do not worry about the stain, unless it would show.

There is a video to help you with this process at:
http://youtu.be/fGNg21bfb2A

Practice Makes Perfect

You should practice until you are comfortable with your strokes, dots, and drops. Also practice removing them. Try different tools to make different sized strokes and dots. Some people find that a certain size tool works better for them and is easier to use. Make sure that you try both ends of each MJ Wax Design Tool.

Know that each Crayola color will work differently. The darker colors contain more pigments and will make bigger strokes because they are thicker. The thinner colors, like yellow, will be thin, but you can pull the stroke farther. Learn the colors and how they work. Thinner colors can also drip a little more. Take the colors that you want to use and pull them with each tool so that you know how long that color will pull and what size stroke it will make.

Practice until your strokes become consistent in size. The more you practice, the better your strokes will become. Remember to load the tool in the well in the same way every time. If your strokes start to get smaller, check the crayon level in the well.

Remember that you are your own worst critic. If you do not like a stroke, then remove it. If it bugs you, take it off.

There is a good video that helps you with all the basics and is a good refresher course at:
http://youtu.be/cR5Tmi-kJ5E

How to Clean the MJ Wax Design Tools

Cleaning your MJ Wax Design Tools is easy. Simply take a paper towel and wipe off the tool while it is still warm. You will need to do this before you use a new color. It you let the wax harden on the tool, removing the wax becomes difficult. Place your tool back into the wax to warm it again and wipe it on the paper towel. I keep my paper towel folded into fours, making it easier to use.

How to Clean the MJ Melting Pot

1.

To change colors or clean your melting pot, simply take a cotton ball and pull it in half. Keep it in balls.

2.

Take the first half of the cotton ball and place it into the well. I use the MJ Wax Design Tool #0, because it can get into tight corners. Do not touch the metal with your fingers. The metal is hot. Using the wax tool, slowly push the cotton ball into the well. If you push the cotton ball too fast, the color comes out the sides, making a bigger mess. Going slower allows the wax to absorb as it goes. Lift the cotton ball out with your wax tool. Start at the front of the well, get under the cotton ball, and pull it out.

3.

Take the other half of the cotton ball and, using the wax tool, clean off the top part of the well. Finish by cleaning the inside of the well. You will be amazed how easy it is to clean. The cleaning is done while the melting pot is still plugged in.

    Once you have cleaned the well, you can put your new color into the well to melt.

4.

The crayon can be left in the well and used again later. Just plug the melting pot back in when you are ready to use it and wait for it to melt before you start. If you are done with the color, unplug the melting pot and let the color cool. When the wax is hard, plug the melting pot back in. It will start to melt on the sides. This happens very fast. Take your hobby knife and push it between the top of the well and the color will pop out in a block.

    You can reuse the color block. It never goes bad. Just pop it in a bag and use it next time. To reuse it, start by adding the block of color to your melting pot first then add any additional wax needed to fill the well.

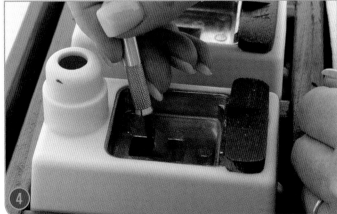

There is a video to help you with this process at:
http://youtu.be/FKQKi-Y9lhs

How to Clean the MJ Texture Brush

1.

To clean your MJ Texture Brush, start by melting the crayon in your brush on the insert.

2.

To clean the MJ Texture Brush and Insert, wipe the insert while in the melting pot with a paper towel.

3.

Set the MJ Texture Brush on the insert to melt the crayon. Wipe the MJ Texture Brush on the paper towel. Keep repeating until the crayon is melted out.

4.

To clean the brush completely, spray with a degreaser like Awesome®. Clean the brush again on the insert in the melting pot until all the color is gone. Rinse with warm water.

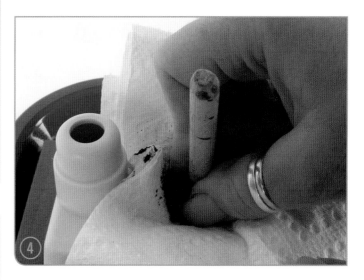

There is a video to help you with this process at:
http://youtu.be/qwwYk4_agoE

Basic Wax Designs

In my first book, Wax on Crafts, I went into a lot of the basic designs. For your benefit, I am revising some of those designs that you will be using for projects in this book as well as the holiday designs. I will be teaching you other ways to use the wax in varied chapters and how to add more color to your designs.

Tips ✓ ✓ ✓

- Remember not to go over a stroke if you do not like it or the size. Remove it and start again.
- Another rule is not to cross over the top half of a stroke. The wax is thicker there and you are running into cold wax. You can cross over the bottom half of the stroke where the wax is thinner.

Basic Shapes

Circles

Out of all my artwork, I use circle designs the most. There is something about them. So the best place for me to start for you is with a circle.

1.

Using the MJ Craft Templates, large circles, pull out the two smallest of these. Lay them down on your paper one inside of the other. Hold them in place with your hand. Trace the inside circle with a pencil.

2.

Remove the smallest remaining template, while still holding the second template in place. Now trace around the inside of the second template.

3.

With your pencil, place a dot in the center of the circle. You are going to pull your stroke from the circle to the dot.

4.

Use the small end of an MJ Wax Design Tool #1. Starting on the inside circle, pull the stroke toward you until you reach the center dot or run out of wax.

5.

Turn your paper around, so the stroke is now on the bottom, and pull the next stroke from the top, again to the center dot.

6.

You have divided the circle into half; now divide it into quarters. Move your paper around a half turn and pull the stroke toward you to the center dot.

7.

Repeat on the other side.

8.

I always do circles by dividing them. It keeps the strokes more even. Now that you have done four strokes, divide the circle into eight strokes. Start by going in between the strokes that you just did, right in the middle.

9.

Complete your circle by always going to the right. This helps you to keep your place and not lose a stroke. You should now have a circle with eight strokes. Turn your paper with each stroke so you are always pulling from the top to the middle.

10.

If you had a smaller circle, you could stop with eight strokes. But to really fill the space and give it a great design, put a total of sixteen strokes in this design. Start again, in between the last strokes.

11.

Continue your strokes around the circle, remembering to go to your right. Turn the paper so that you are pulling each stroke toward you. With a little practice, you will have a nice circle. Make sure that you are

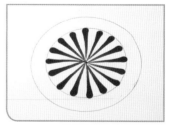

setting your hand completely down and resting it on the paper to give you the most control over the stroke. Now try bigger circles and smaller circles. Change the tool for the size stroke you need. Try different color crayons, see how they pull differently?

There is a video to help you with this process at:
http://youtu.be/zxw6f8pZwbg

Double Circles

Take your circle to the next level by turning it into a double circle. This will teach you how to build on a basic design. Switch to the MJ Wax Design Tool #2 small end. This helps fill up the pattern. Most people do not think that the stroke will fit between the smaller strokes. The fattest part of the stroke is above the smaller circle.

12.

Start at the second circle and pull the stroke down between each stroke. Pull the stroke until it runs out of wax or you reach the center. Do not worry if you run into the wax on the smaller circle.

13.

Complete your strokes by going to the right, moving your paper so that you pull the stroke from the top toward you. You should have a total of sixteen strokes in this second row.

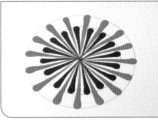

14.

To clean up the tails of the strokes in the center, add a dot to the center. You can pull strokes out from the circle; you can add dots or descending dots. How do you see the design? What can you change or add? If you do a very small

circle in the center, you may want to work with the circle on the outside first. Then complete the smaller circle. This would keep the smaller circle cleaner.

You can use this method and apply it to any shape including squares, diamonds, and ovals. It makes the design less overwhelming if you break it down. It also helps keep the pattern more even.

Freehand Designs

Fleur-de-Lis

Once you have gotten shapes down, let's work on a little more freehand strokes. You cannot pull a stroke across the top of a stroke because the wax is cold and hard. You can, however, pull a stroke into a stroke and combine their tails. Start with the simple fleur-de-lis.

1.

Pull a stroke down the center. If you need to draw your lines on to follow, do so with the white charcoal pencil or regular pencil. These lines will be covered with your stroke, so you will not need to remove them.

2.

If you want a larger design, use a larger tool; if you want a smaller design, use a smaller tool. I am using an MJ Wax Design Tool #2. Pull a stroke from the right and meet up with the first stroke about halfway down, then pull the stroke into the end of the tail. Repeat on the left side.

3.

Easy right? Now you are going to add on to that. Pull a stroke along the bottom right of the design, the tail meeting up with the design in the center. Repeat that stroke on the left side.

4.

Add another set of strokes above the bottom ones. Start the set just a little closer to the center than the one you just did. Pull it until you meet up at the center end. Repeat the stroke on the left side.

5.

Dots add so much to a design. Finish this design off by adding descending dots to the top of the first stroke. Then clean up the design by adding a dot to the bottom where the tails meet.

There is a video to help you with this process at:
http://youtu.be/sP9xooAWlOk

Crashing Wave

1.

Start your stroke by pulling it curved over and down. The next stroke will start near the top of the prior stroke; curve it over and down just like the last one. Continue adding strokes until you have completed the area you need to fill.

2.

As always, you can add dots. I have placed my dots inside the design. You can place them above the design or in both places.

These basics can add so much to a project. Start with the basic designs and build on them. Put some of them together.

There is a video to help you with this process at:
http://youtu.be/Y9liiwqB9Fs

Rolling Wave

1.

If you need to draw the basic design with a pencil and follow it with your tool, that is okay. Start a stroke by setting it down and curving it to the right, then left and pull the tail out, coming back toward the middle. If you do this stroke in the other direction it creates an "S." You may find one direction easier to do than the other direction. Each stroke should start in the curved part of the tail in the stroke above it. The more you practice, the easier it will become.

2.

To complete this design, add dots to it. You can add the dots on the top right of the design, or add them to the left of the design, or both.

There is a video to help you with this process at:
http://youtu.be/Fh-DdR_QBk4

Leaves

Basic Leaf

You are going to learn some different leaves that you can use by themselves or with flowers (changing the whole look of the flower). Different colors in a leaf can change the color of it as well.

Heart Leaf

Let's move on to a fancier leaf. This is my favorite leaf. It can add a lot to a simple flower. Keep this leaf in mind if you have a bigger space that you need to fill in.

1.

Starting with green wax, using the MJ Wax Design Tool #2 small end, pull a stroke out from the right side curving around and pulling it until it runs out of wax. Pull a stroke out from the left side curving it until it runs out of wax, meeting up with the first stroke.

2.

Change the color to yellow green. Switch to the MJ Wax Design Tool #1, pull the stroke starting at the top of the leaf, and pull until you run out of wax near the tip of the leaf. You can create a leaf just like this.

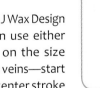

3.

Switching to the MJ Wax Design Tool #0—you can use either end, depending on the size you may want the veins—start at the top of the center stroke and set your tool down. Pull your tool up and out. This helps give you a smaller stroke with a point. You are not pulling the stroke the whole way out unless you have room. Continue adding small strokes down the center stroke and repeat on the other side.

There is a video to help you with this process at:
http://youtu.be/esPy-e3eFg0

1.

You are going to start at the opposite direction for this leaf. Pull your first stroke in, beginning where the leaf will end. Make sure you allow enough room for the leaf. Pull the stroke until you run out of wax. The size of the wax tool you use depends on the size you want the leaf to be.

2.

Starting on the left side, start the stroke a little from the top and pull the stroke out toward the left, curving down, and pull until you meet the tail of the first stroke.

3.

Now go to the right side and repeat. The two strokes that you just made should look like a heart.

4.

Pull the next row of strokes the same way, except you will pull these out a little farther then you did the last ones. This makes your leaf fatter.

5.

Continue with the rows on the leaf until you fill in the space or you are running out of wax before you get to the center stroke.

There is a video to help you with this process at:
http://youtu.be/qKzUlCvetxY

Holly Leaves

Another leaf that I use a lot is a holly leaf; it is great for Christmas projects. The tool to use would depend on the size you want your leaf.

1.

Start on the left side and curve your stroke in toward the middle and back out. It should have a backward "C" look to it, but not as curved. You can draw the pattern first if you need to.

2.

Start at the same spot as you did for the last stroke. Pull a curved stroke in the other direction giving it a forward "C" look.

3.

Start at the bottom of the stroke on the left side. Pull the stroke the same as you did the first one, giving it a backwards "C" look.

4.

Start at the bottom of the stroke on the right side. Pull the stroke the same as you did the first one, giving it a forward "C" look.

5.

Start at the bottom stroke on the left. Pull the stroke inward toward the middle of the leaf. Pull it until it runs out of wax, giving it a sharp tail. Do the same for the right side, meeting up with the tails in the middle.

6.

To give the leaf a more dramatic look, change the color of the center vein. On the inside of the leaf, pull the vein down the center from the top where you started.

7.

Finish your holly leaf off by adding red descending dots to the top.

8.

Build on this holly leaf by adding another one. Place your new leaf behind the first one. Starting on the right, just below the top of the first holy leaf, pull a curved stroke out.

9.

The left side will mostly be covered by the first leaf. The next stroke will be below the one you just did, again pulling a forward "C"-like stroke. Pull this a little farther out to the side.

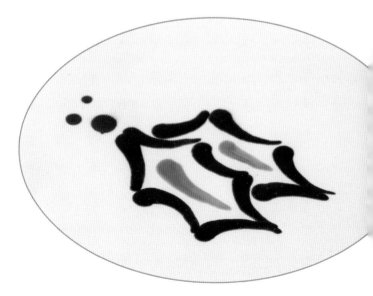

10.

The last stroke on the right side again will be at the tail of the prior stroke. Pull a stroke with a forward "C" look, but end your tail more where the middle of the leaf should end. Make sure you pull that stroke with a long tail.

11.

Pull a stroke in from the bottom left side like the leaf is coming from behind. Join the tail of this stroke up with the tail of your last stroke.

12.

Pull a center vein down the leaf. You could do a leaf on the left side, too, if you want.

There is a video to help you with this process at:
http://youtu.be/VC7_-A5r2EE

Flowers

Little Rose

1.

To make the rose a little easier, start with a basic drawing. Draw a dot in the middle and a line coming in from the left side curving around the dot. Draw a line coming in from the right side followed by another one coming in from the left.

2.

Since this is a small rose, use a smaller tool. If you want it bigger, use a larger tool. Start by pulling the first stroke in from the left. Stop the tail at the end of the line you have drawn.

3.

Just underneath the tail of the last stroke, pull a stroke in from the right.

4.

Go back to the left side and pull another stroke in from the left to complete the rose. Keep the strokes close together to make the rose look like a rose. Add a dot to the center top of the rose.

5.

Changing to a green color for the stem, pull a stroke using a larger tool from the center bottom of the rose downward. Pull it nice and slow so that you get a nice long stem.

6.

Pull a stroke from each side of the center stem. These strokes can be a little smaller. They are the leaves for the rose. See how sweet and simple that was?

There is a video to help you with this process at:
http://youtu.be/R0BTeP61vi8

Large Rose

1.

Start with a dot in the center of the rose. Using a smaller tool, pull three strokes close around the dot. Flower petals are usually in odd numbers so to make your flowers more pleasing to the eye, try to create flowers with five and seven petals.

You can draw your pattern first if you need to boost your confidence and to assist with placement. Just for an example of size, I used a larger tool for the center dot and used an MJ Wax Design Tool #0, large end for the first row.

2.

I used an MJ Wax Design Tool #1 large end for this row. Learn to adjust for the size of rose you want. Put five strokes around the rose. Keep the strokes close to the first row of petals.

3.

Move up to a larger size tool and create the next row of petals with six or seven strokes. Keep the strokes close to the previous row of petals. I used an MJ Wax Design Tool #2, small end, for this row. I did

not worry about which direction I pulled my rose petals. You can, however, pull them going a different direction, starting at the middle of the rose. This makes it look like it is blooming from the center. Play with that. Find what you like. Do not be afraid to find your own style.

4.

Now pull a green curved stroke out from the side of the rose. Pull the stroke until it runs out of wax. I used an MJ Wax Design Tool #2, small end, for the leaf.

5.

Pull a petal from the other side of the leaf. Pull it until you run out of wax while joining it up with the tail of the other stroke. Move your paper or project so that you are pulling the petal toward you. It is easier to pull a stroke toward you.

6.

Now pull a stroke down the middle to complete your leaf.

This is the basic leaf. Use leaves to fill in where you might have a hole or gap in the rose.

There is a video to help you with this process at:
http://youtu.be/NnbzchQUaxs.

Sunflower

You are going to create a sunflower using simple strokes.

1.

Start with a center for your flower. I traced a circle using the MJ Craft Templates. The size of your tool will depend on the size of your flower. Pull a curved stroke out away from the center, until you run out of wax.

2.

Pull the other side of the petal from the center of the flower. Curving the stroke, meet up with the tail of the stroke you just made. (This is also a basic leaf pattern.)

3.

Start your second petal next to the one you just completed.

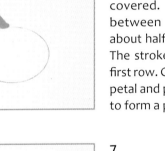

4.

Continue the petals all the way around the flower. Try to have an odd number of petals.

5.

Starting at the circle, pull strokes down the center of the petals. You could use a different color, like orange, if you want contrast.

6.

Now do a second row of petals. Start about halfway up the petals of the first row. Your bottom half of this petal is covered. Pull the stroke in between the first row and about halfway up the petals. The stroke is taller than the first row. Go to the other side and start the stroke on the other petal and pull until you meet up with the tail of the first stroke to form a petal.

7.

Continue all the way around the first row. You can add just a few petals here and there, or add a third row. Do what you think is right.

8.

Now add center veins to the second row. Start down in between the first row of petals and pull it to the top of the petals.

9.

Start adding your leaves. Use them to fill in spots that are empty. Start your leaf coming out from the first row in between the second row of petals. I like to make these leaves larger than the petals. Sunflower leaves are much bigger than the petals.

10.

Continue to add a few more leaves. Remember to add them in odd numbers. You can add them to just the top of the flower, just the bottom of the flower, or all the way around. Decide if you want a vein down the center of your petal, or whether you want smaller strokes for more veins.

11.

The center of the sunflower is made with descending dots. I use a larger tool and start by adding dots. Do not let the dots in the first layer touch until they are cool. If warm wax meets warm wax, it runs together and you lose the shape of your dots.

12.

On the second layer of dots, I used a different color. This gives the flower some depth. On a sunflower center you could use black or brown dots.

Start thinking about how you would do it differently next time. What colors would you use? By simply changing the color of a sunflower to red, you now have a poinsettia. To give it a little Christmas sparkle, add little gold wax dots to the center. What other flower could you create by changing the color? How about using the wax liner and adding a swirl to it? What would happen if you made a different colored flower and added heart leaves instead?

Have I got you thinking? It is my mission for you to take what I am teaching you and build on it. Come up with your own designs and style!

There is a video to help you with this process at:
http://youtu.be/4_ooQnux-jk

Cosmos Flower

1.

Start with a circle in the middle. You can draw your flower petals on if you need to. Start at the top center of the petal. Pull the stroke curved around and down to the flower center. Repeat on the other side of the petal forming a heart. If your wax is still warm at the top of the petal, it will form together. That is okay for this design.

2.

Complete the petals all around until you form the flower. Leave a little room in between each petal.

3.

Try different strokes or dots inside the flower petals. I did descending dots down the middle of the petal.

4.

I decided that there was still room in the petals to add a small stroke on each side. Would you like the petals with the strokes and not the dots?

5.

Try a dot on the top of the petal where the strokes meet.

6.

Instead of a dotted flower center this time, do a circle design. Pull your strokes one at a time from the circle to the center of the flower. Divide the strokes to form a circle. Add a dot in the center. Do you like this center better? What other types of centers for flowers can you make? What colors would you like to try?

7.

There is still a lot of room in between the petals. Pull a stroke from about the same height as the petals, in between each of the petals to the circle center. That changes the whole look of the flower.

8.

To give it more of a whimsical feel, add some more dots. Take the descending dots out from the top middle of the flower petals. Do you like it with or without the descending dots? What would you do differently next time? What type of leaf do you feel it needs? How can you put a flower behind this one?

Have I got you thinking yet? This is a great example of starting simple and building on it. Take what you have learned and make it your own.

There is a video to help you with this process at:
http://youtu.be/8A6moTrX4Gg

These make great presents. Do a set of six or more for Christmas presents, fall or Halloween decorations, birthday presents, or favors for a wedding. I have also used the half-inch tiles with a holly design for Christmas. Do you give Christmas pictures at Christmas time? How about sending decorated tile magnets to hold the picture on a refrigerator door?

Decorated Tile Magnets

1.

Start with a simple project, one that is easy to handle and flat, like a ceramic tile. Use an unsealed tile. You can use sealed tiles as well; just make sure that you use a thick varnish to keep the wax secure. For this project I used 2" tile.

2.

If the tiles are unsealed, you may need to seal them with a coat or two of spray varnish. The best way to know if you need to seal a tile is to pull a stroke on the tile. Did the stroke come out smooth? If the stroke is broken or was hard to pull, seal the tile. I used a spray varnish from Krylon® gloss to seal the tiles. It is inexpensive and dries fast. Put two coats of varnish on and try the stroke again. If it pulls smoothly, you are ready to apply the wax.

3.

Here is a holly design. You can use any of the designs from chapter four. This holly has a leaf underneath the center leaf on both sides. It has just a little white wax added with an MJ Wax Brush. Dip into the white crayon and pounce the wax out, meaning go up and down with your brush until you have the amount of wax you want. This gives it that Christmas spirit.

There is a video to help you with this process at:
http://youtu.be/NgZvnleTti4

4.

Make Christmas tiles with poinsettias. Remember the sunflower? Just change the colors up. I used red for the flower petals, yellow-green for the leaves, brown and yellow for the center dots, and added three black descending dots to fill in space and to give it a little more festive feel. The flower is off center. Put the center of the flower in a corner and start from there.

Pumpkin Magnet

So, I want you to try a design that we have not covered to learn how to create your own designs!

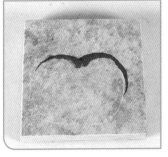

2.

Start again at the top center; pull three strokes down filling in the pumpkin and creating the ridges. You can do more strokes if you have more area to fill. Keep the number of strokes odd so that you have a stroke in the center of the pumpkin.

3.

Start at the bottom center; pull a stroke up on the left side and one on the right side. This creates the bottom of the pumpkin.

1.

To create a pumpkin, start by drawing a basic outline. Allow room at the top for leaves and a stem. I used an MJ Wax Design Tool #1, small end. Starting at the center top, pull the first stroke to the left following the pumpkin shape until your wax runs out. Adjust to a bigger tool if you need to pull the stroke out farther. Start at the center top and pull a stroke following the pumpkin shape on the right side.

4.

With brown wax, create a stem. You can play with making a stem. For longer stems, pull strokes next to each other while the wax is still warm, so the wax will melt together.

5.

Put "simple (basic) leaves" on the top of the pumpkin with yellow-green wax.

6.

See how the pumpkin still looks kind of plain? It needs to be filled in a little more. Start by adding a few more strokes from the bottom of the pumpkin, meeting up with the strokes on the top. That is better.

7.

The top still needs to be a little more filled in. Add another leaf to the right.

8.

To brighten up the design, add some highlights in the pumpkin using a dandelion-colored crayon. This really helps to fill in the design and give the pumpkin more depth.

9.

There are also a few open areas that could use a little something. Fill those in with three descending dots. You can use one dot in areas where three will not fit. This just really helps complete the design and gives it a magical fall feel.

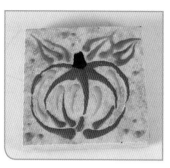

See how you created a basic design and filled areas in that need something more? You've learned you can add more strokes to a basic pattern if needed. Leaves make great fillers. Use lighter colors to create highlights in the pattern. The three descending dots can complete and add so much to a pattern. What else did you learn?

To make a magnet out of the design....

1.

...take one of the prominent colors used on the design and find a matching acrylic paint. Paint the sides of the magnet. I sealed my tiles with epoxy resin. Place the tile on something that elevates it and the resin can run off the sides. I used a "Popsicle" stick to spread it around and make sure all the areas were covered. Wipe any resin off the bottom of the tile. Make sure that all the wax—especially dots because they stick out higher—is completely covered with the epoxy resin. Allow to dry. By covering it with resin, it is waterproof, heat-proof, and hopefully drop-proof.

2.

Allow the resin to dry. Glue on a heavy-duty magnet with E6000®. Make sure you glue the right side of the magnet to the tile. E6000 is a great glue for hard-to-glue items, like rock, glass, plastic, and so on. Allow the glue to completely set for twenty-four hours.

Rose Heart Ornament

Handmade gifts mean so much to people, who realize that you cared enough to do something special. I love to create special items for people who may be overlooked on Valentine's Day. Something so little can mean so much. This little rose heart ornament is the perfect thing. Simple, inexpensive, and quick to make, this is my Valentine's go-to gift. Start with a heart ornament.

1.

I found a red, glass heart-shaped bottle for Valentine's Day.

2.

Decorate with the rose bud design.

Make several hearts and turn them into a Valentine's wreath. Put the roses on heart-shaped candy containers.

You can use the wax technique on Christmas ornaments, clear or colored plastic, or glass. The possibilities are endless!!

3.

Add descending dots to the design to complete it. Change the color of the rose to pink or yellow. Add swirls instead of dots. To seal the ornament, I used 3-D Crystal Lacquer®.

There is a video to help you with this process at:
http://youtu.be/jcOJevnP4dl

There are several Valentine's projects on my YouTube Channel at:
https://www.youtu.be.com/user/Miriamjoy123.

Love Potion Bottle

I found a red glass heart-shaped bottle at my local Dollar Store around Valentine's Day.

1.

Starting at the top left, pull a curved stroke to start the foundation of your design. You are going to be freehanding this project without any patterns. (This gets you thinking about what you can add and how to fill the area, as well as how to create your own designs on the project you have.) Add several other curved strokes to complete the top section. Pull the strokes in the design where you think they should go. You can pull the strokes together by joining them together in the tails. If you think a spot needs a stroke, add it. Does it fill that space well?

2.

Move to the middle section of the bottle. Continue adding strokes to the design.

3.

Complete the bottom left section of the bottle. Do you feel that it has enough strokes?

4.

Add a little swirl design to the right side. You may feel it needs more design or less. What about just adding descending dots?

5.

Complete the design by adding dots to it. The dots really finish the design. Dots can be used to fill in areas that need a little "something." I sealed this project by brushing on 3D Crystal Lacquer.

6.

Take pieces of pink colored paper and write "love notes" to your special someone.

7.

Curl the pieces of paper by wrapping them around a pencil. Place the notes into the heart.

8.

Find a plastic jewel or diamond that is big enough to sit on the opening of the bottle. Tie a ribbon around the neck of the bottle.

There is a video to help you with this project at:
http://youtu.be/D8z5HDb_P5I.

Instead of love notes, you could fill the bottle with hearts or candy, or use it for a centerpiece. You can also turn the bottle into a candle holder.

There is a video to help you with this project at:
http://youtu.be/uQ2Rs54R_qM

There are lots of inexpensive colored bottles. What designs can you add to them? Have a holiday coming up that you would decorate them for? You could also color your own bottles and put designs on them.

Great gifts do not have to cost a lot. Most of my projects start with a trip to the local dollar or thrift stores. It is amazing what you can do with simple items and a little wax.

I picked these cute little frames up from the craft store. I paid a dollar each for the frames and the Valentine's stamp pad. I loved the bright shiny colors and the style of the frames. I thought they would be really cute as a holiday decoration.

Heart Frames

1.

Open up the back of the frame and pull the insert out. Trace around it on a piece of paper with a pencil so you know what size you will be working with.

2.

With the stamp pad and in the color of your choice, stamp the Valentine's stamp in the center of the piece of paper. If it is not in the center, try again, or stamp your design on and then trace around the stamp with your frame insert and cut it out to make sure you have the design where you want it.

3.

Using a dry sponge, rub it into the ink to pick up the color and rub the sponge around the outside of the paper to give it color. If you want more color toward the center of the design, pounce a little more color with your sponge until you are satisfied.

6.

Glue embellishments on the frame with E6000. The embellishments give the design a personal touch. In this case, it added more of a romantic feel.

7.

I created the white frame in the same way, but instead of a wax tool, I used the MJ Wax Liner over the stamped design. I then added a few more swirls in the corners. I completed decorating the frame by gluing on a rhinestone linked chain around the inside of the frame.

There is a video to help you with this project at:
http://youtu.be/TKyPTtkgIqE

The idea is to add color to a stamped design. Bring out some of the details to make the design stand out. It brings it to life. You are creating a framed piece of art in very little time, hardly spending any money. I cannot wait to try a Halloween design with orange and purples and pull wax strokes over the pumpkin designs! Thanksgiving designs with names on the bottom for seating place cards would be super cute for that special meal.

4.

With a small wax tool, fill in the tiny hearts in the jar giving the hearts a puffy look. Do one side of the heart at a time; set the wax down like a dot and pull with your wax tool to form a tip. Load your tool and pull another side of the heart while the wax is still warm on the first side, so the wax will run together to form one shape.

5.

Spray the design with a non-yellowing spray varnish and put it back into the frame with the clear plastic on the outside of the design.

...Things to Think About...

- What color frames can you find?
- What stamps do you have? Make them for all the holidays—like Christmas, Halloween, Thanksgiving, a baby shower, a wedding, and the list goes on.
- You could also use colored pencils to color some of the stamp design.
- Create a frame without the stamp and just a little design done in wax.
- Put a person's initial in the frame.

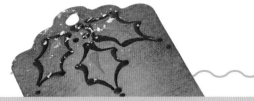

Since I was a little girl, I have loved to wrap presents. This worked out great for my mom. She would bring me some wrapping paper, ribbon, and tags and I would spend hours in my room creating the most beautiful wrapped presents I could think of. So, of course I would love to make my own tags to give presents that wonderful personal touch. Sometimes the package is the best present.

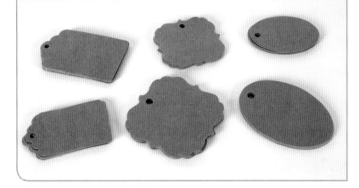

1.

I found all kinds of shapes and sizes of thicker brown tags at my favorite craft store. You can find them in the scrapbooking section, too.

2.

Pick out a stamp pad color that you want for your tags.

3.

Rub your sponge oin the stamp pad to pick up the ink. With your sponge, run the color of the ink along the edges of the tag, giving it some much-needed color. If you want to keep the tags plain and rustic looking, use a brown stamp pad.

It is easier to make several tags at one time, by doing that you have one ready when you need it.

4.

Add designs to the tags. I followed the design of the tag most of the time. You can use the rolling wave design or the sunflower (poinsettia) design. The holly leaves are still one of my favorites. Fill in with dots or little fleurs-de-lis. You can make tags using one color or you can decorate with several colors. You could also make tags with just dot designs.

    Think of the times you might need a tag. Would it be for Christmas or maybe someone's special birthday? Once you start making them, you will not want to stop.

I have several little Christmas patterns to help if you need it at:
Miriamjoy.com

    You can write a person's name with a pin on the tag or use the MJ Wax Liner. Just make sure that you use a color that will show up. Black is always a good choice, unless your background is dark.

    Finish tags up by spraying them with your varnish—this is not a heavy varnish, so be careful to keep the tags out of the direct sunlight.

There is a video to help you with this project at:
http://youtu.be/uHdWXV17aqQ

...Things to Think About...

- What events are coming up where you might use a tag for a present?
- If you are getting married, do you need special, elegant tags for your bridesmaid's gifts?
- To make the tags more masculine, keep with browns and blacks.
- To make the tag really rustic, dip a fan brush (shaped like a fan) into water and then into black acrylic paint, with another brush, hit the fan brush in the middle of the handle, making little black dots. You could also use this technique with any color you wanted.

Poinsettia Candles

Everyone loves candles, especially for the holidays. They do not have to cost a lot and are wonderful gifts for all the people on your list, including all the people at the office. They can be colored or plain.

I love to use candle holders to give height to the piece and to make the candle look more elegant. Placing different candle holders together with varied heights makes a great arrangement. You can also stack the candles holders together. Glue them together with E6000. Let the glue dry for twenty-four hours before moving.

1.

Take an ivory-colored candle and add a sunflower design to it. Use red wax to turn it into a poinsettia.

2.

Use dandelion for the center dots...or what about using brown with some metallic gold dots?

3.

The heart leaves are a yellow-green color. You could change the leaves and use green for the outside and yellow-green for the veins.

4.

Complete the design with three descending dots using dandelion color to fill in the design. You could use the metallic gold for fun and to give it a more festive look.

I spent around $3.00 on this candle and stand. To make it brighter and more festive, I would like to add a big red bow to the middle of the candle holder.

Holly Candles

You can also take plain candles and add your own color to them. Purchase long thin candles. They do not have to be white; you can use any color candle for a color base.

1.

To paint these candles use red, metallic gold, and metallic red acrylic paints.

2.

Start by wetting a craft sea sponge. Wring out all the water from the sponge. Lightly dip the sponge into the red paint. Pounce some of the paint off until you get a nice even coat of paint. Pounce the red paint onto the candles. Let the top part of the candle dry before you try to do the bottom part where you are holding the candle. You will take the paint off or smear it if the paint is not dry.

3.

Lay the candles on the MJ Dry Board until the paint is dry. This allows the paint to dry on all sides and not stick to the board.

4.

Once you have paint on the entire candle, let it dry, then pounce gold metallic paint onto the candle. This layer of paint is not as solid as the last layer; you want to leave room for the next color. After that layer is dry, repeat with red metallic paint.

5.

Starting at the top of the candle and working your way down, put on a holly leaf with green crayon wax. Since you are making smaller leaves, use a smaller tool.

6.

Change to yellow-green and pull a stroke down the center of the holly leaf.

7.

Add three red descending dots for the berries. Start with a holly leaf on either side of the candle. Move down and put holly leaves in between the two above. Try to turn the leaves so that they are not all facing the same direction.

8.

In an empty melting pot, place the insert on top of the well. Once the insert is warm, melt some white crayon evenly across the top of the insert. With the MJ Texture Brush, pounce into the wax and then apply some white wax to give it that Christmas sparkle. Put the white on the tops of the holly leaves and any area that needs a little more color.

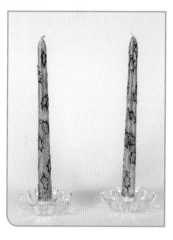

9.

If it is easier for you to work on one candle at a time, do that. It may be easier for you to work on both of them at the same time especially if you are working with one melting pot. You can do the outside of the leaves first on all of the candles, then the yellow-green down the center. Put all the holly berries on and then use the MJ Texture Brush to put on the "sparkle." Varnish with spray varnish to brighten up the paint and wax.

10.

Set in candle holders and add a bow to really make them pop. Give them as gifts. Instead of wrapping them, tie them with a big red bow.

I've also created Valentine's candles on red thin candles with little white hearts to create that special mood.

There is a video to help you with this project at:
http://youtu.be/bbynb3MTjWI

There is a video to help you with this project at:
http://youtu.be/bbynb3MTjWI

...Things to Think About...

- What color do you want to make your candles?
- What wax designs would you like to add to them?
- What holidays are coming up that you could make candles for? How about red, white and blue for the 4th of July? What if you made a special candle for a special birthday?
- How about different layers of candlesticks to change the height of the candles?
- What other items besides bows can you use to put on the candlesticks?
- Add candles to a basket with floral items to make a great centerpiece.

Candy Heart Box

There are so many great boxes today. For example, what about the heart-shaped boxes that contain those wonderful chocolates we all love. Why throw the box away? Turn it into a new treasure box or give it as a gift. Paint the outside of the chocolate box with red acrylic paint. You may need a few coats of paint.

1.

Using the MJ Wax Design Tool #2, small end, add a rolling wave design around the edge of the box with white wax. Starting at the middle of the heart, do the design in one direction on one side and the opposite direction on the other side.

2.

Start with an oval shape. Draw it on with your white charcoal pencil. Still using white wax, add a cosmos flower to the middle of the box. Do two strokes on the inside of the petals and one dot on the inside of the petal where the top strokes came together. You can draw the petals on first if you need to.

50

3.

There is a lot of open area that you need to fill. Add a leaf made up of strokes. Start with the stroke the farthest out, and work your way toward the flower. Use black wax for the leaves to give them a more dramatic look.

4.

Add strokes down both sides of the center stroke to form the leaf. Do two more leaves in the open areas of the box. Still using black wax, put descending dots in the center of the flower.

5.

Add descending dots to fill up more of the area on the leaves. Add black dots to the rolling wave design around the outside of the box. Descending dots were also added to the center of the leaves to clean them up. Three white descending dots were used to complete the design on the top of the box. Then add a fleur-de-lis to the top middle where the rolling wave designs meet.

6.

I did not paint the bottom half of the box because it had these great colors on it. I did add a rolling wave design in black with dots around the white edge sticking out.

7.

If you've made any mistakes and had to remove a stroke or needed to clean up the design, paint back over it with the base color that you used. You can also use this to cover up any lines you may have drawn on.

8.

I use a triple-thick brush-on varnish, which is a heavier coat of varnish for this project. I did two or three layers of varnish.

Glitter Snowflakes

During Christmas I fill my house with snowflake decorations. I love the "sparkly" feeling they give you. The wax design technique on a snowflake can add so much. You can add whatever color you like. The snowflakes could be red and green. I prefer the blue and purple to give it more of that frosty feel.

I love to use wax designs on glittered snowflakes. The possibilities are endless. Glittered snowflakes are abundant and pretty inexpensive. The first thing you should do with an item that is covered in glitter, even if you are not going to put wax on it, is to spray gloss varnish on it. This keeps the glitter on those items for years to come. If not, the glitter is more likely to fall off and the surface underneath becomes exposed.

1.

To begin, follow the shape of the snowflake. Pull a stroke down the middle. Then add strokes on the sides. You do not have to know the whole design in advance. Just start and the design will come to you.

2.

In areas that are bigger, add more strokes. But it does not have to be strokes—it could be dots. Work your way around the snowflake.

3.

Instead of always going in the center of the design, outline the design with your strokes. Change colors in certain areas of the snowflake to change the design. Use some metallic or glitter crayons for a different look.

4.

Stack your snowflakes. This creates a new look and makes them more 3-D. You can find smaller plastic snowflakes with several in a package.

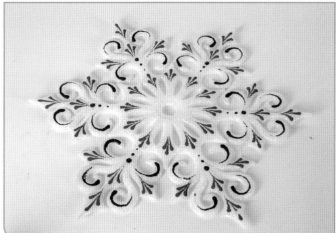

5.

Try several different types of snowflakes. Some are on cardboard or wood-like backing, while others are made of plastic.

6.

Keep the smaller snowflakes simple. Do not overdo it. Sometimes less is more. You can add to the design by using different colors.

Snowflake Centerpiece or Vase

Do not think of snowflake ornaments just for hanging on trees. Consider what else we can do with them. Let's turn that ornament into a great centerpiece or vase.

1.

Start with a glass cylinder vase. Glue a matching ribbon around the vase with a hot glue gun.

2.

When gluing on items with the wax design with a glue gun, you must set the glue gun to a low temperature! A hot temperature will melt the wax.

3.

Make sure that you have varnished or sealed your snowflake before you glue it on.

You can fill your vase with anything you want—flowers, pine cones, or Christmas bulbs. Keep it or give it as a gift. The total cost of this project was about $2.50. Can you believe that can make something this nice for that price?

The nice thing about this design is that you can remove the ribbon and tuck the snowflake away until next year. The vase is ready for the next holiday.

Another way to add more to the snowflakes is to glue on pearls or rhinestones along with the wax design. See how simple the wax is on these snowflakes and how much elegance it provides by adding the pearls. People pay a lot of money for store-bought items as pretty as these. Add ribbon to the candlesticks to display the snowflakes in a different way.

There is a video to help you with this project at:
http://youtu.be/6u8QB0NEVw8

When decorating words, follow the shape of the word; start from the outside and work your way to the middle. Use dots in between strokes to fill in the area. You can also use a center stroke and a stroke on each side of that. See how changing colors on those strokes gives the design so much more color and festivity?

The bigger glitter word looks great with all the fun wax designs. The bigger the word, the more design you can add to it. I just get so excited with all the possibilities.

Do not get stuck thinking just snowflakes. There are many other items you can work with, like this blue glitter reindeer. Add wax to bring out the design in the reindeer. I tied a bow matching the one on the vase around his neck and glued the reindeer to the ribbon on the vase.

There is a video to help you with this project at:
http://youtu.be/dUKT9bcj9jI

Use the words together with a bigger project. Combining snowflakes and "joy" with ribbon and Christmas picks makes a fun little wreath.

There is a video to help you with this project at:
http://youtu.be/2VAWyUl6wbQ

I use the "peace" words in my Christmas tree. I have about ten of them scattered throughout the tree. This helps fill in any empty spots and gives my tree a whole new dimension.

To match my tree, I also put them on wreaths for my doors. Using the layered snowflakes and the "peace" word is now one of my favorite decorating techniques.

There is a video to help you with this project at:
http://youtu.be/faghsbVhtnQ

...Things to Think About...

Do not get stuck in just Christmas. I know I showed you a lot of snowflakes and Christmas designs. There are a lot of other holiday designs done with glitter. Check your local dollar store or holiday section in your favorite store for glitter items that you can decorate. There is Easter, Halloween, 4th of July, and New Years to name a few.

Think of other ways to use them:

- Remove the ribbon and replace it with wire.
- Make some loops in the wire and add some beads.
- Add a ribbon to the wire and maybe some flower picks.
- If you want it more country-looking, add a stripe of material or burlap for a bow.

When you are working with twice-melted wax, always work on a tray with a layer of paper towels to keep the area clean and absorb any melted wax. Make sure you have an apron on.

You have learned that you can put wax on a candle, but what if you wanted to melt the colored wax a little more?

Halloween Candle

1.

Start with an inexpensive red candle. Put black crayon into your well to melt. This is one of those times that you can have the wax higher than the well if you want. Set your glass eyedropper into the well and let the glass warm. Squeeze the bulb of the eyedropper and fill up the glass tube with wax. Do not overfill the eyedropper. Try not to get wax up in the bulb. It is really hard to use the eyedropper if the wax hardens in the bulb. When you are done with the eyedropper, make sure you squeeze the bulb really well to get out as much wax as possible.

2.

With black wax loaded into the eyedropper, drop a line of black wax down the side of the candle. Do this by squeezing the wax out. Squeeze the wax until you get the line as long as you want it.

If you have enough wax, go ahead and start the next line of black wax. Reload when you run out. You may like to reload the wax each time.

3.

Keep space between the black lines. Go all the way around the candle. Try to make the lines different lengths. The lines will get longer when you melt them (step 6). Pick up the candle from the bottom, to keep your fingers out of the warm wax, and move it around so it is easier for you to reach.

4.

Once you have gone all the way around the candle, bring some black lines in from the top outside of the candle to the middle, near the wick. Line it up with the lines on the sides. Do not do every line. The wax does not have to be perfect.

5.

Now that you have the black wax around the sides and top of the candle, you are going to remelt the black wax. You will be using an embossing gun or heat tool. The embossing gun can be found in the scrapbook section of the craft store. (Remember to use a coupon!) You can also use a blow dryer on the high setting, but it will blow the wax around more.

6.

Start to heat the black wax a section at a time. Heat the black wax until the drip at the bottom is melted. The more you heat the black wax, the more it will spread and flow farther down the candle. The closer you hold the embossing tool to the candle, the more it will melt the wax. If you want to melt it less, hold the embossing tool farther away from the candle.

7.

Make sure to heat the black wax on the top of the candle as well. If you want the wax to melt down, blow the heat down with your embossing tool. If you want the wax to melt to the sides, blow the wax to the sides with the embossing gun.

8.

If the wax melted and left an area that needs more wax, add more black wax to that area with your eyedropper. Heat the wax that you just added. Make sure that you do not overdo it, which would result in not having enough red showing.

9.

Heating the wax also helps clean up any areas on the candle that were torn up or where the wax was not smooth. Heat the candle and keep adding wax until you like the look of the candle.

There is a video to help you with this project at:
http://youtu.be/XisvXk_JfCI

Things to Think About...

- What would this look like if it were a bigger candle?
- How about orange wax on a black candle?
- What happens if, while the candle is still warm, you add glitter to it?
- What other colors could you use?
- Would this be fun for other holidays?
- How would the look of the candle change if it was put on a tall glass candle holder?
- Should fall leaves be added to the candle holder?

A Red, White, and Blue Example

Here is another example of the same melted design.

1. Use a red, blue, a little white, and a silver crayon. Melt the same way as the prior candle.

2. Add extra-fine white glitter to each section as you are heating the candle. Add glitter to the top of the candle.

3. Pick up a glass candle holder, glass star candle holder, and candle, 4th of July necklaces, and 4th of July garland.

4. Glue the candle holders together with E6000.

5. Cut the garland into eight sections and wrap them around the middle of the glass candle holder. Twist it tight to secure the garland, then wrap each end around a pencil to give it a curl.

6. Place the candle in the middle of the star and put the necklaces around the candle.

This project cost me a little over $5.00 to create. It was so easy and fun to make.

There is a video to help you with this project at:
http://youtu.be/YibqcTnvn4s

I started with a glass cylinder vase. This vase has a heaver bottom so it is great for gluing onto a tall candle holder. This vase has a heavier bottom so it is great for gluing onto a tall candle holder.

1.

For this project, you will be using red crayon. Heat your glass eyedropper and fill it with red wax; start by dripping the wax from the top of the vase. Let the wax come about a third of the way down. It will come down a lot more once it is melted.

2.

Bring the eyedropper back up and put a little row of red wax between each red drip. If the vase has a little ridge at the top, try to start the wax under that ridge. Continue all the way around the candle holder.

5.

I used 3D Crystal Lacquer to seal the wax. I poured the lacquer into a plastic bowl and put it on with a paint brush. I then allowed it to dry.

3.

Heat the red wax with your embossing tool. Try to keep the tool pointed down so the wax will melt going down. Make sure to melt all the drips until they lay flat. **WARNING: DO NOT TOUCH THE GLASS WHILE IT IS HOT!**

6.

Take a cardboard toilet paper tube and cut it with scissors about one third of the way down from the top of the vase.

4.

Heat the wax all the way around the vase. Remove any drips from the base of the candle holder with your hobby knife. Remove any wax flecks that may have gotten on the glass.

7.

Fill the toilet paper tube up with tissue, paper, or a plastic bag almost to the top of the roll. Leave just a little room so that you can later place a flameless votive securely on top. With a hot glue gun, glue the bottom of the tube to the center of the vase.

8.

Fill the empty space between the vase and the tube with red glass stones. The toilet paper tube should not show. I found plastic hearts in a bag at Valentine's and used those. The hearts give it a more romantic feel.

9.

Place the flameless votive on top. **DO NOT USE A REAL CANDLE.** Do not glue the candle in because you will need to be able to turn the candle on.

10.

Do not fill the vase so full with stones or hearts that you cannot see the candle.

A Red, White, and Blue Example

Here is another example of the candle holder using the prior method. Instead of one color of wax, I used red, blue with a sliver of white added, and white crayons. Be careful when you melt the blue and red next to each other; blended, it makes black. It may work better if you add white wax between the red and blue wax. I added silver glitter to the top of the vase while I melted each section. I used the 3D Crystal Lacquer to seal it. I added the star garland to the bottom candle holder and set a silver glitter flameless votive in the middle. You could use the toilet paper tube the same way here and use colored stones that match. See how different it can look by changing the wax colors?

...Things to Think About...

- Would you like it more if you added hearts or heart garland to the center of the tall glass vase?
- What about a big red or silver bow with a heart in the middle?
- Could you make this for your friend using their favorite colors?
- What colors of glass stones can you find and how will that change the look?
- What if you melted the wax on the star vase?
- How would it look if the glass were colored?
- What other holidays can you do this for?

You can always change the look of the candle by gluing the vase to a tall glass candle holder with E6000. If you knew that you wanted to glue it on, you could do so before the project. Remember to let the E6000 set for twenty- four hours before moving it.

There is a video to help you with this project at:
http://youtu.be/C05Z6pnqzKw

Now you are going to take the twice-melted wax to the next level! You have learned how to apply the wax on in sections, but, in this next project, you are going to learn how to apply and melt solid wax layers to create a wonderful rainbow effect. You will be working on an egg that has had the yoke blown out. There are also other egg-like products you can use. At Easter time, there is an egg that looks like an egg and dyes like an egg, but has a plastic inside, making it less fragile. There are also egg gourds—a type of gourd that grows in the shape of an egg. They are hard-shelled making this my favorite to use. Egg gourds can be bought from gourd farms that can be located on the Internet.

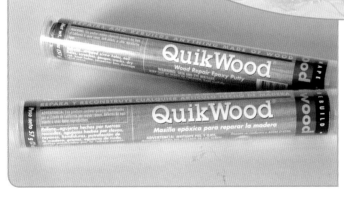

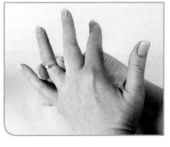

1.

Start by creating the hanger for the egg. This is very important. You cannot use glue because you are going to use heat on the egg and that will melt the glue and would make the hanger fall off. So this next step is very important. You are going to use QuikWood as your glue to hold the egg to the bead cap securely.

I treat QuikWood like clay. What I love about QuikWood is that you have thirty minutes workable time and it dries rock hard in an hour. I mean rock hard.

2.

The first thing to remember when working with QuikWood is to remove all of your jewelry—because rock hard means rock hard, even if it's in your jewelry.

3.

Spray your hands with a vegetable spray. This keeps the QuikWood from sticking to them.

4.

Take the QuikWood out of its container. You will find the manufacture's instructions. Please check all the precautions. Remove the metal foil circle on top.

5.

QuikWood is a two-part epoxy. It is premeasured. All you have to do is mix it to activate it. You can see the equal parts in the picture. One part is tan and the other part is white.

6.

With scissors, cut a very small amount. Make sure you take a big enough piece to get equal parts of the epoxy. This will be enough for several eggs. Place the metal foil circle back on top of the roll to help keep it fresh. If you are all done with the QuikWood, put it back into the plastic roll and put the lid back on it.

7.

There is a plastic wrap around the roll of QuikWood. Do not remove the plastic until you cut a small piece. This keeps the rest of the QuikWood fresh. But you do have to remember to remove the plastic off the smaller piece. (I cannot tell you how many times people forget and cannot figure out what is wrong with the clay when they find that there is a piece of plastic in it.)

8.

Knead the two parts epoxy together to activate the QuikWood. This step is very important. If you forget to knead it together or do not knead it enough, the clay will not harden.

9.

Knead the clay until all the marbleizing is gone and it becomes one solid color. It will start to become warm to the touch.

10.

A bead cap is exactly what the name says it is: it is a cap that goes over a bead. You can find the bead caps in the bead section of your craft store. Pick out at least a 16-mm to 18-mm bead cap with a hole of 4 mm or larger. The hole has to be big enough for your cording or string to fit through.

11.

Cut a piece of cording the size you want the hanger to be. Match up the tails of the cording and loop them around and pull the tails to form a knot.

12.

Run the cording through the bottom of the bead cap. If the cording is too big for the hole, try wax linen, fishing line, or thread.

13.

The knot should be big enough that it does not go through the hole. If not, tie another knot or glue it in. Make sure the knot will fit inside the bead cap.

14.

Fill up the bead cap with a small amount of QuikWood. It shouldn't extend past the edges of the bead cap. This is a very small amount.

15.

Push the bead cap onto the top center of the egg. Hold up the egg with the string and see if it is centered. If not, move the bead cap around until it is.

16.

With your hobby knife, remove any QuikWood that squished out the bottom of the bead cap. If there is a lot, use less on the next egg. It is easier to do several eggs all at one time. Allow the QuikWood to dry for one hour.

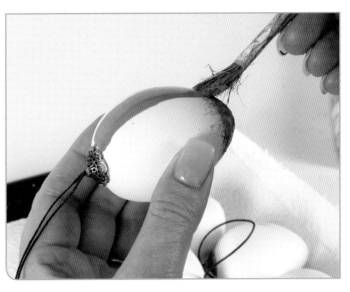

18.

Using a different brush for each color, dip the brush into robin's egg blue and do a stripe down both sides of the egg. The wax does not have to look even. Do not go back over the wax while it is warm. That pushes the wax around and makes it uneven and harder to melt.

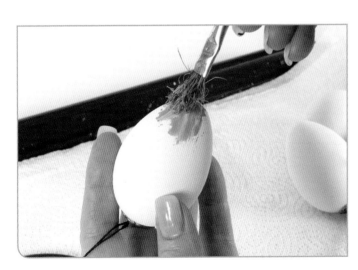

17.

Once the QuikWood has hardened the fun part begins. Put the crayon into the melting pot. This is one of those times that you can have the wax fuller then the top of the well. With an MJ Wax Brush, dip into your melted wax to pick up the color you want. I started with yellow-green for the bottom of the egg. The bottom of the egg is going to be covered by the rest of the wax that melts down, but you still need to cover the entire egg with wax for it to melt evenly.

19.

Next, put a pink carnation stripe right next to the robin's egg stripe. Make sure that you do not have any uncovered part of the egg between the two colors. If so, take the brush with wax and fill that area in.

20.

The regular crayons give the egg its bright color, but a little metallic color gives the egg the shiny sparkle. Do not use more than one or two metallic colors on the egg—the egg will start to become dull in color. The metallic color that I used for this egg was cyber grape.

21.

To really brighten up a design or project, use dandelion yellow. It really makes the colors pop. The dandelion finished the coverage of the wax on the egg.

22.

Work on a tray with paper towels in the tray to absorb the drips of wax. You will get lots of drips. I placed a paper towel folded into fours right under the egg. I am using a plant hanger that I found at the craft store or plant section of a store. It screws tight onto the table and holds the egg secure. You could also use a smaller ornament hanger as long as the egg does not touch the hanger.

23.

With your embossing tool, start heating the top of the egg. Go around the bead cap and get the wax melted and moving down. It is important to remember that the wax will continue to melt while you are working on other sections so do not overheat it.

24.

Once the top is heated and the wax is moving down, move down to the next section of the egg. The wax should become smooth and even. Do not overheat the wax; stop when the wax becomes shiny and even all over the egg. If you overheat the egg, most of the wax will drip off and the colors will be blended more, making a muted or brown color. You can always heat it more if needed.

25.

If you have an area that has too much of one color in it, use your eyedropper and put a line of another color down the solid color.

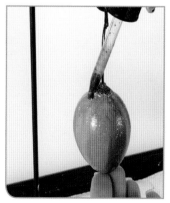

26.

Reheat that area until the egg is smooth. Do not be afraid to try different things on the egg. If you do not like the look, melt the wax on the egg and wipe it off with a paper towel, then start again.

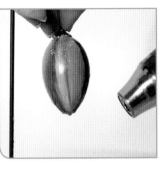

27.

You will notice a drop of wax at the bottom of the egg. When you are done melting and have the wax where you want it, while the wax is still warm, touch the drop of wax with your finger and gently remove it.

28.

You can also add glitter to the egg— to the top, or a section, or color of wax. Just make sure the wax is warm enough for the glitter to stick. I really like to put tensile glitter (longer strands of sparkly glitter) into the wax to give it a different look. You will not want to stop with one egg!

You can also use the MJ Wax Design Tools to apply the wax. This method takes a lot longer, but the wax goes on thicker with the same result in the end.

There is a video to help you with this project at:
http://youtu.be/Ue9-4B9xwmQ

Decide what method—varnish, or sealer—you would like to use on the eggs. One of the methods that I like to use with eggs is gloss varnish in a can. I dip the egg up to the bead cap and hang it on the hook over the can so it can drip back in. You get a good thick even coat of varnish. Keep the egg on the hook until it is dry. I do at least two to three coats.

...Things to Think About...

- What happens when you put the wax around the egg in stripes going around, not up and down?
- What other designs could you try? Try heating your wax tool and moving the wax around.
- What types of glitter do you have and how would that look in the design?
- Try micro beads instead of glitter.
- Use the twice-melted egg as your base and add a wax design on top of that.
- Could you make orange and purple eggs and put a Jack-o'-lantern face on with black wax with a wax liner?
- Christmas ornaments made out of eggs with red, green, and gold would be beautiful on a tree.
- How about adding a red or gold bow on top of the egg?
- How about blue, white, silver, and purple for a winter ornament?

Glass Christmas Ornaments

For this next project you need to find an ornament hook that you can hang a glass bulb on, so you can heat it without having to hold the bulb. Make sure that the bulb is glass, not plastic. The plastic will melt. I like different shapes of ornaments beyond just the round bulbs.

1.

Remove the ornament hanger from the top of the bulb. Turn the bulb on its side and squeeze colored wax into the bulb with your glass eyedropper. Work with one color at a time. Try to keep the colors separated. (If blue goes over red, it will make black.) Put a lighter color between the dark colors. Keep turning the bulb as you apply the color. Only have the drips of wax go down half of the bulb or less. The wax will move down when it is heated. Do not put too much wax in the bulb. Too much will flow to the bottom and form a chunk of wax with ugly colors.

2.

Once you have put the wax into the bulb, heat it with the embossing gun. Use a leather glove to move the glass bulb around. **Warning: The glass will get very hot! Do not touch the glass with your bare hands!** Start at the top of the bulb; when the wax starts to melt, move down. Make sure that you turn the bulb as you go so that it heats evenly on all sides. Do not overheat the bulb. You can always reheat it some more, if needed. It will melt very fast.

3.

If you want to have the wax swirl around, you can do so by just moving the bulb around. I leave mine more vertical.

For more ideas, see the videos for Christmas, Easter, fall, and snowflakes ornaments at:
www.youtube.com/user/Miriamjoy123

A Red, White, and Blue Example

Make a 4th of July ornament with red, white, blue, and silver. You can add a little glitter to the wax while it is warm. The glitter will not show up as much, because it is on the inside. Since the wax is on the inside, you do not have to varnish the ornament when it is done. Just put the ornament hanger back on the bulb.

...Things to Think About...

I display my ornaments on different-sized glass candle holders. If you go to a thrift store, you can usually find different heights, whereas if you go the dollar store, they are often the same size. Add a red bow for color.

- How pretty would it look to do a whole row of ornaments on top of the fireplace mantel at Christmas?
- Use different shapes of ornaments too.
- What would a whole glass vase full of the ornaments look like?
- How about a table centerpiece with several ornaments on the glass candle holders with an evergreen wreath around the outside?
- What if you used the colors blue, purple, white, and silver instead?
- How about using glass bulbs at Easter for some colorful eggs?
- Try adding a wax design on the front of the glass with the twice-melted wax in the background.

You have been learning how to manipulate the wax into designs. How about putting the wax designs into jewelry? This project is so simple and fast that you will not believe it.

1.

Start with a metal pendant blank that you find in the jewelry section or scrapbook section of your craft store. Make sure the pendant has sides that come up to hold the wax in. I prefer the ones that are a little deeper because they hold more wax. (I also carry them on my website at www.miriamjoy.com to make sure that you have them available.)

2.

On this necklace pendant, I decided that I wanted to use Christmas colors so I had something nice to wear for the holidays. Everyone loved it and I had to make a lot more for Christmas presents.

Heat the glass eyedropper in the melting pot well with the red wax. Squeeze the bulb to bring the wax up in the tube, but not into the bulb. Squeeze the bulb a few times to get as much of the wax out that you can out when you are done with a color. Put red wax in a couple of places in the pendant.

3.

Use a different glass eyedropper to add dandelion to give the pendant that bright accent color. Make sure to fill the pendant up to the rim but not above it.

4.

Know how many colors of wax you are using. Make sure you have an eyedropper for each color if possible. You are using one for each color because they are hard to clean. If you do not have one for each color, squeeze the bulb out as much as you can, and use a similar color, like green and yellow-green in the same eyedropper.

5.

Add yellow-green to the pendant. It brings in a lighter color so the pendant does not get too dark. Make sure to leave enough room for all the colors you want to use.

6.

The last color is metallic sunburst. It is going to give the design sparkle and a festive look. You can go over some of the other colors that you have put in. Remember to keep the wax below the rim of the metal pendant. You may need to add more wax in the middle if the wax goes down low within the pendant.

10.

Work your way around from the sides, in circles that touch, until you reach the center. You should have a nice thick coat on the necklace. Make sure that all of the wax is covered so that it will be heatproof if worn in the hot sun. Do not move the necklace. Let it dry in this place.

7.

Heat your pendant until it starts to get warm; stop and warm your wax tool. Since this is a small area, use a smaller tool, like the Wax Design Tool #1. You can also have your tool sitting in an empty melting pot to warm. If the tool is not warm, the wax will stick to the tool and not move the wax well.

8.

Warm the wax again until it is liquid and you can move the wax around with your wax tool. This is a smaller area, so do not pull the wax too much. Sometimes less is more.

This necklace is done with dandelion, yellow-green, carnation pink, metallic sunburst, and just a touch of robin's egg. While the wax was still warm, I put micro beads on the top of the necklace and heated that section just a little more. Like the projects prior, you can add any type of glitter you may like to the wax while warm. I would try to just do a section or a color. Doing the whole pendent with glitter may be too much.

I have several designs for necklaces and ornaments at:
www.youtube.com/user/Miriamjoy123

...Things to Think About...

- What colors would you like for the necklaces?
- Would you like glitter in your project?
- Would you like fewer colors?
- How about red, white and blue for the 4th of July?
- What other holidays can you do?
- How about using two metal pendants and turning them into earrings? There are also metal pendant bracelets.
- Turn them into ornaments instead of pendants. They would be great to hang on a tree.

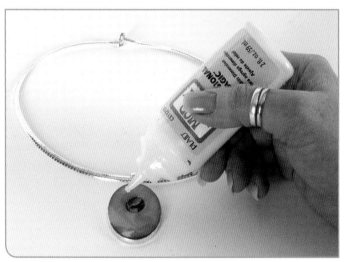

9.

When the wax is cooled, which takes a matter of seconds, seal the wax with Mod Podge Dimensional Magic®. Start on the outside of the pendant and apply a thick coat of Dimensional Magic.

Favorite Fall Projects

I love Halloween and fall. I love all the rich, bright, warm colors. You can feel the crisp change in the air. But my favorite decoration is the pumpkin. It takes me back to a magical time when my kids were little and excited about the season. We use to all go in our Halloween costumes to the pumpkin patch to find the perfect pumpkin. My daughter could not get enough pumpkins. She would ask everyone she knew for a different kind of pumpkin: big ones, little one, yellow ones, and orange ones. She named every one of them. But she said that everyone got the name wrong: they should be called "plumpkins." My beautiful little girl brought the magic to the season, so to me a "plumpkin" must be magical.

Magical Pumpkin

What is more magical than a glittered pumpkin? You can find them at most stores in the Halloween or fall section of the store.

1.

As mentioned previously, the first thing you should do when you buy an item with glitter on it is to spray it with spray gloss varnish—no matter what the item is. This not only helps keep the glitter on, but also helps makes the wax go on a little more smoothly.

2.

Work on the top third of the pumpkin. Nature is usually odd, not even. It is more appealing to the eye if designs are odd, reflecting nature. That applies even when dividing an item. It is less pleasing to the eye if the design was divided in the middle. Start by putting a thick line of tacky glue toward the middle of the pumpkin. Do two to three lines on each ridge of the pumpkin. The lines should all start at a different layer. Do not make them all even. Apply a line of glue in the creases of the pumpkin. Take your finger and spread out the glue. If you did not smooth out the glue, it would be harder to apply wax later and take longer to dry.

3.

Continue around the pumpkin. If the glue is drying too fast, you can work with one section at a time. When I work with glue or glitter, I always work on a tray with a layer of paper towels. That keeps the mess confined. When I am done with the glitter, I can just trash the paper towels with the glitter. It helps keep everything else from becoming a little "sparkly."

4.

For the glitter, I used polyester glitter which is very, very fine. Shake it onto the glue-covered pumpkin.

5.

Allow the glue to dry very well. You can spray-varnish the pumpkin again if you like. This helps the wax pull smoothly and keeps the glitter that you just put on in place.

6.

Use purple crayon with just a little white to create the purple color. Using the Wax Design Tool #2, the small end, add three strokes to each gold glitter section around the pumpkin.

7.

Using the same tool, add three descending dots starting at each gold glitter section moving toward the bottom of the pumpkin.

8.

With the glass eyedropper, drop dandelion dots around the center of the pumpkin for some more color. Let dry and then add orange drops in with the dandelion drops.

9.

Decide how you want to seal or varnish your pumpkin. For this project, I would use Triple Thick spray varnish. Go with what would work best for your needs and what you prefer.

10.

When I was working on this project, there were no fall leaves at the craft store. But, I found a batch of fall leaves hiding with my decorations, begging to be re-purposed from a box of last year's fall decorations.

11.

Now this is a magical pumpkin, so your leaves need to have that magic, too. Paint them with gold Extreme Glitter® acrylic paint. If you do not have glitter paint, you can put the tacky glue on your leaf and sprinkle it with a little gold glitter. The paint just combines both steps into one. Let the leaf dry.

12.

Take your scissors and cut the leaves into the shape and size you want. Make three leaves: two big leaves and one smaller one for the top part of the stem.

13.

Use the wax liner to add wax veins to the leaves. I used dandelion and red crayon colors, but you could use any color that you want with your project—like purple, orange, or brown. This brings out more detail to the leaves. When finished, you would never guess they were plain fall leaves to begin with.

14.

Glue the two leaves onto the stem above the pumpkin so it gives the leaves some height rather than laying them flat down on the pumpkin. Glue the little one near the end of the pumpkin stem.

There is a video to help you with this project at:
http://youtu.be/QU_tfpXhTQo

15.

To add a little more to your pumpkin centerpiece, take a garland wreath and place your magical pumpkin in the center.

...Things to Think About...

Think of all the ways you can add so much more "magic" to your fall decorations.

- **What colors can you see on your pumpkin?**
- **What other colors of glitter could you use?**
- **How about using a couple layers of glitter?**
- **Instead of using the wax design tool to apply the wax, what if you used the MJ Wax Liner to create lines?**
- **What different leaves could you put on it?**
- **What if you made three different sized pumpkins for a centerpiece?**
- **What drama would it add if you put the pumpkins on glass candle holders?**

I love baskets. They remind me of a much simpler time. When I was a little girl picking berries with my aunt and cousins always involved a basket; so did picking flowers from my grandmother's beautiful garden. You may have a basket with dust on it stuck in a closet somewhere. Baskets are always plentiful at the thrift stores or you may come across one that you just have to have at the local craft store.

Look for a basket with only one rim in the middle for this design. Seal the basket before you begin, with a spray varnish to make the wax pull evenly without penetrating into the fibers of the basket. If you are uncomfortable with doing this, do a test stroke on the bottom of the basket to see how the stroke pulls. Even if it pulls nice you might still do a spray varnish first. This helps the wax come off without absorbing and leaving a stain if you need to fix a mistake. If you want the basket to have a matte look, use a flat varnish.

1.

Divide the top half of the basket, into three sections. The sections here turned out to be an inch apart. I used the MJ Flex-e ruler to measure because it can bend and be placed flat on any object. I only worked on the top or front sections—not the sections that sat behind.

2.

Using the circle Mini MJ Craft Templates, find the circle that fits the width of the section of basket you are working on. Place the template so the top of the circle starts where you marked. With a white charcoal pencil, mark on the template where the circle stops. This way you can use the same part of the circle for all of the design.

73

3.

Then trace the inside of the circle. Make sure your template fits and does not fall off the section you are working on. If it does, you may need to move to a smaller size template.

4.

Move the template to the middle section where the markings on the template line up with the first circle. Trace the circle; stop when it meets the circle you just drew. Move the template to the top section and repeat. If you are using a bigger basket, you may need to add more. Complete this pattern around the top of the basket.

5.

Flip the basket over and repeat the same on the bottom half. I only had room for two circle designs. You may have more, depending on the size of the basket.

6.

Use a wax tool that applies wax all the way down from the top of the circle to the center of the circle without running out. I used dandelion for the center stroke. Stop the stroke if you start to go into the next circle. Decide if it is easier to complete all of the dandelion strokes first on the basket or if it is easier to complete the entire design on each section. If you are working with only one melting pot, do all of the dandelion first, so you do not waste the wax.

7.

Switching to orange crayon, pull two strokes on each side of the dandelion stroke until you reach the center. Make sure you are pulling the strokes to the center at the tail of the dandelion stroke, not just straight down. If you pull the strokes straight down, you will get more of a shell look. You can place a dot there if you need a reference point.

8.

Complete this on the rest of the design, or do a section at a time, if you decide it is easier. Use the same wax tool for the entire project.

9.

Switching to red crayon, pull the remaining strokes from both sides of the circle to the center. You may have to adjust how many strokes you pull. I only had room for three strokes on the last section. With this design, try to have at least three strokes. You may need more if your sections and basket are bigger. Complete the rest of the design or section.

10.

I found that it was easier for me to do the top half first and then do the bottom half of the basket.

11.

You might have to adjust the bottom circle on the bottom half of the basket because of the rim around the middle.

12.

I felt that it needed a little simple design on the middle rim. I kept it the size of the section. Use the same tool, pull a black stroke from the side to the middle of the section above.

13.

Now turn the basket over and pull the stroke from the other direction. The strokes should meet in the middle.

14.

Pull a stroke on each side of the center stroke you just did. The tails should all meet up in the middle. Make these strokes a little shorter than the middle stroke.

15.

Flip the basket over and repeat on the other side.

16.

Put a black dot in the center to clean up the strokes and make the design complete. You could do this on the bottom rim. If you did it on the top rim, you have to be careful where the handles go over the rim. The handle could knock the wax off or scratch it. Finish the basket off by varnishing or sealing it. I used Triple Thick brush on; you can seal the whole basket or only the sections with wax on them. Do at least two to three coats.

...Things to Think About...

- What other type of baskets do you have?
- On dark baskets, use light or bright color wax; on light baskets, use darker-colored wax designs show up better.
- What if you added flowers to the basket?
- How would it change it you added leaves to the flower design?
- You could decorate the basket with poinsettias and put Christmas bulbs in it for a holiday center piece.
- Holly leaves might be fun and festive.
- How else could you decorate the basket for the different holidays?

1.

In this project, start with a foam pumpkin. The brown wrapping paper I found in the shipping or mailing section of the store and I also picked up the brown wrapping paper there. It is usually found in the shipping or mailing section. You want the paper to be a heavier weight so that it does not tear easy or fall apart. Use regular Mod Podge to apply the paper.

2.

You are going to be using acrylic paints, metallic paints, and glitter paints for this project.

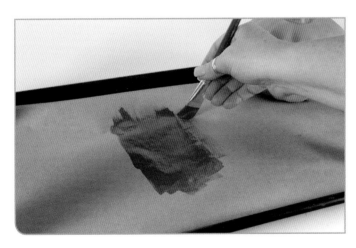

3.

Decide how much brown paper you need for the pumpkin. It should be one and a half times larger than your project. It is better to have too much than not enough and have to repaint the paper again. (I wrapped the paper around the pumpkin to get an idea.)

Work in a tray, so you do not have to worry about making a mess.

Start with a tomato spice acrylic paint. This is a darker red than bright red. Use just a little water in your paint so that it makes applying the paint easier. You can add the water to the paint. Start with a little and add more water if needed. It is easier to add more water than more paint.

Use a flat brush or a base coating brush to apply the paint to your paper. The first layer of paint should be solid. You only need one layer of red.

4.

Next apply pumpkin acrylic paint. Wet your craft sea sponge and wring out as much water as you can. You do not want water in the sponge to water the paint down.

Put the pumpkin color into a paper plate and pull the color out onto the plate with your sponge. Pounce the sponge into the pulled paint on the plate. Pounce the color onto the red. You want quite a bit of orange (pumpkin) color, so that the pumpkin appears orange.

5.

Do the same with a school bus yellow. Pounce less yellow onto the paper. This is the highlight color. Turn your sponge as you are pouncing color so you do not get the same exact pattern on the paper.

6.

Make sure to sponge the edges of the paper just like the middle, so that you have color there. Allow the paper to dry.

7.

Spray the paper with a good coat or two of Krylon spray varnish. Allow the paper to dry very well. This is really important. The paper must be dry so it will not to stick to itself in the next step.

8.

Take the paper and start to crumple it up.

9.

Crumple the paper up as hard as you can with your hands. This makes the lines that the crayon will go on. Do not do this in smaller sections of paper because you will get to many smaller lines.

10.

Once you have pressed the paper really hard with your hands to form the creases, unfold the paper. Do not press the paper flat.

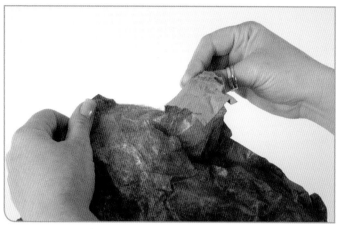

11.

Tear the strips into two-inch sections. You can tear all of the paper or just a section at a time as you are working. Do not use scissors. You do not want straight lines.

12.

Now tear the strip again into two-by-two-inch sections. It is okay if they are different sizes. This size is just faster and easier to cover the area of the pumpkin.

13.

With your hands roll the Mod Podge to mix it. Shaking the bottle creates bubbles. Pour the Mod Podge into a container and apply with a flat paint brush. I save my old brushes for things like this.

14.

Start by applying the Mod Podge to the pumpkin. Only do a section big enough for your paper. It will dry out too fast if you try to do much more.

15.

Generously apply the Mod Podge to the back of the paper. Applying it both to the pumpkin and the paper makes it stick better.

16.

Pick up more Mod Podge with your paint brush and apply over the top of the paper. Make sure to get the edges pushed down.

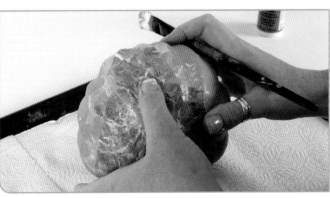

17.

Overlap the pieces of paper on the pumpkin. Make sure that you do not have any open areas of the pumpkin showing through.

18.

Continue to apply paper to the rest of the pumpkin. Do not worry about the stem. Just bring it up a little on the sides; you will cover the stem later with paper twist.

   Do not worry about the Mod Podge being white. It will dry clear. This is the one time that you do not have to worry if you have creases in your paper.

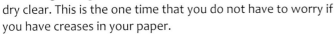

19.

Let the pumpkin dry. You can see the brown lines where the paper shows through from tearing it. I think this just adds texture to the design.

20.

Pick a crayon color that goes well with your design. I picked purple. It has to be a color that really shows up and does not blend in with the background. Remove the paper from the crayon. You'll want a larger piece, but small enough that you can hold it between your fingers. Heat the crayon in the middle with the embossing gun. Do not heat your fingers.

21.

When the crayon starts to melt, rub it on the pumpkin. The crayon will come off on the ridges that are sticking up from the pumpkin. When the crayon gets cold and does not leave much color, reheat the crayon and start again. The warmer the crayon, the thicker the wax it leaves behind. The colder the crayon the less wax it leaves.

22.

Continue to heat and apply wax to the pumpkin until you have an even color of wax applied.

23.

Seal the wax with another coat of Mod Podge. Brush it on the entire pumpkin and set the pumpkin on the dry board. Let the pumpkin dry.

24.

See how many pieces of paper twist you need to go all the way around the pumpkin stem. I used two pieces.
• Cut the pieces to about six to seven inches in length.
• Untwist the paper twist.
• Cut the top part with scissors to form a sharp point.
• Re-twist the top part.
• Leave the bottom part un-twisted.
• Glue the paper twist pieces onto the pumpkin stem with hot glue. Make sure the pieces overlap each other.
    The leaves were done using the same process as the Magical Pumpkin.

25.

The stem to me was awfully plain. So I added gold glitter paint to it. You could also create this effect with glue and fine gold glitter. Just do not add too much glitter.

26.

Glue the leaves onto the pumpkin. You can use any kind of leaves that you would like with this project. You may like green leaves better.

An Example Using Gourds

I used this paper process on two gourds. I used turquoise acrylic paint for the base coat on the turquoise gourd and sponged metallic gold and copper metallic paints. I melted black crayon for the accent color. I put a leather strip around the turquoise gourd and glued a stone on top of the feather.
    For the purple gourd, I used a purple paint base coat and sponged a light purple, orange and a metallic gold paint. I melted robin's egg for the accent color. I glued a string of beads on top.

There is a video to help you with this project at:
http://youtu.be/82u1KzXH5Fo

...Things to Think About...

• What other colors of paint could you use?
• What about a black pumpkin with orange wax?
• Apply dark leaves with bats or ghosts to the stem.
• What would it look like on a bigger pumpkin?
• What if you sponged the pumpkin color and yellow on after the paper was applied with Mod Podge onto the pumpkin? You could create better ridges that way.
• How about doing a frame with the paper and wax process?
• What other wood items do you think you would like to try?
• How about applying the paper process to one of the big plastic Easter eggs in spring colors?
• How about a papier-mâché box with Christmas colors?
• Make a wooden frame with colors of your choice.

79

9

Adding More Color to Your Wax Projects

In this chapter we are going to talk about how to add more color to your project or wax designs

Making a Pattern

In this chapter we are going to talk about how to add more color to your project or wax designs. You can turn any design into a pattern. Take the design and break it down into strokes. Use a bigger tool for a bigger stroke and a smaller tool for a smaller stroke. If the design has a solid line you may have to break it into a couple of strokes.

There is a video to help you with this project at:
http://youtu.be/J3G3rB7EdGE

If you need help, I have a lot of patterns available on my website at Miriamjoy.com to help you add the perfect design to any project.

Break a pattern into strokes.

Pumpkin done with wax strokes

How to Trace a Pattern

To trace a pattern onto a project, use a sheet of black or white charcoal paper, depending on what color shows up best on your project. Check to see that you have the correct side of the charcoal paper down by writing on it and seeing if the line appeared on your project.

Make a copy of your pattern so you always have the original. Place your pattern on top and trace over the lines with a pencil. Make sure you are applying enough pressure to create clear lines that you can see—using a pencil can show you what you have traced. Do not try to trace the stroke, put a line down the middle of the stroke. Your original pattern will give you guidance on which way your strokes are pulled.

There is a video to help you with this process at:
http://youtu.be/az8iAMEDPwA

Draw a line down the strokes to trace a pattern.

How to Float Color

One of the things that I do the most to add to a design is to float color around the project with a darker shade, like brown, to bring the design forward and keep it from fading into the background. It can be called floating color or color blending.  You may also hear the terms "shading" or "highlighting," but that is just referring to a lighter or darker color float. The brushes can also be called shaders.

Start with a bigger brush. You can use a flat or angled brush. The flat brush is a #10 and the angled shader is a ½-inch brush. I have always used an angled brush to float color with, which is my preference. You may find that you prefer one type of brush over another one.

To float color, I use acrylic paint. If you know how to float and use just water—that is great. If you are just learning to float, using a blending medium is much easier. I will be using red acrylic paint so that the float shows up brightly. You need  a surface that is slick to blend your colors on. Make sure you know where you put the medium; it is clear in color and hard to see on the plate. I pour a little of my paint and a little bit of the blending medium on my paper plate. I use a paper plate instead of palette paper. It seems easier to me. The paper plate should be the kind with a waxy coat over it. If you do not have a paper plate or palette paper you can use wax paper.

Wet your brush with water and wipe it on a paper towel. Dip your brush, just a little, into the blending medium. Put your brush onto a clean spot of the paper plate and pull short strokes overlapping each other to blend the medium into your brush.

Now dip half of the brush sideways into the paint. The paint should only be on half of the brush. If you are using an angle brush this should be the longest part of the bristles.

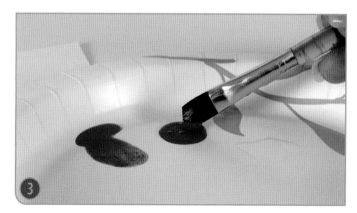

On a clean part of the paper plate, lay your brush down so that all of the bristles are on the plate. Pull a stroke on the plate. If you have loaded the paint too far into the brush, you will get a solid line like the first stroke in the picture. The perfect stroke goes from solid paint on one side of the brush to no paint on the other side of the brush. The color fades out. Pull a couple of strokes until the color is faded out on the outside. You are now ready to float on your project.

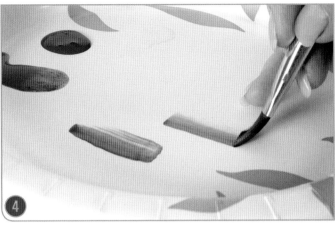

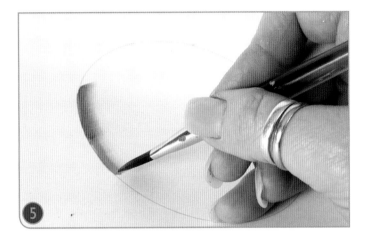

Set your brush down and pull until you start to run out of paint. Stop, then dip your brush back into the blending medium and paint just like you did before. If the brush starts to get color all the way across, rinse out your brush in water and start again. If you are floating with just water, you have to rinse your brush and reload each and every stroke.

Pumpkin with a brown float around the outside

Pumpkin with floating in the pumpkin and leaves

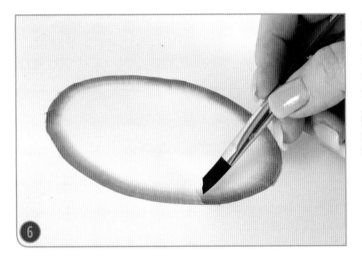

Floating color can be used inside the design as well to highlight an area or shade an area. To make an area look like it is behind another part, float (shade) that with a darker color. To make an area look like it is on top or reflecting light, float (highlight) that with a light color, for example, white or a light yellow.

There is a video to help you with this process at:
http://youtu.be/TLyBB1q3xtc

Once you have reloaded your brush, start where you left off on the last stroke. Floating is different for each type of surface you are working on. For example, you can go back over paper and blend it a little better, but for surfaces, like wood, let the paint dry before you try to go back over a float to blend it or you will just pick up the paint.

Adding Color Washes to Your Design

Adding a color wash is one of the fastest ways to add a lot of color to your design. Since you are adding a wash and not base-coating the design, it saves a lot of time.

To apply a wash of paint to your design, start with acrylic paint: pour a little onto your plate and add a little bit of water to the paint. Mix the paint with the water. It is better to add less water and keep adding then to add too much water.

Brush it onto your project. The wash should be thin enough that you only need one coat. The coat should not be spotty. The paint should be very bright, but still transparent. You can apply your floats for shading or highlighting over the wash for a more dynamic design.

You can apply the wash before you add the wax design, or you may find that it is easier to apply the wash after the wax design. When applying a wash over a wax design, you have to wipe off any wash color that remains on the wax strokes. You can do this with a Q-tip at any time before you varnish your project.

There is a video to help you with this process at:
http://youtu.be/1W8g-76TYyY

Pumpkin with color wash

Pumpkin with color wash and floating

Pumpkin base coated with color

Pumpkin base coated and floating added

Base Coating Your Design

If you want a bright, solid color behind your wax design, base coat it first with acrylic paints.

Put the outlines of your pattern or design on first. Apply one layer of paint at a time. Allow to dry in between coats. Apply as many layers as you need to have the paint one solid color.

Bright red and bright yellow are hard colors to base coat and need several layers of paint. To make it easier, use one layer of a thicker color, like maroon for red, and a straw for the yellow.

Finish base coating with the red or yellow paint. It will take a lot less coats of paint this way.

You might ask yourself: If I painted the design, why do I need to add the wax onto the project?

The wax adds a whole new dimension. Paint is just flat and the wax adds a puffiness or 3D look to the project. Even pictures do not do the project justice because you are still looking at a flat picture.

Trace your pattern back on over the top of the base coat with your charcoal paper, if needed. Add your wax design to the project.

Saw with base coating and floating added

Saw with wax design added

Sleds bring back wonderful childhood memories, waiting for enough snow that you could sail down the hill screaming and giggling with pleasure, jumping off at the bottom of the hill and running up to do it all over again. How many times would you run up that hill before you fell into the snow exhausted? My favorite sled run was in the wash. You would turn to the right or you would hit the cement boulder, turn again to the left or you would go into the sage bushes and jump off before you got to the water or you might break through the ice. If we survived, we would jump up and do it again. My friends and I would take turns and sled all day until our mothers called us in for dinner.

Christmas Sled

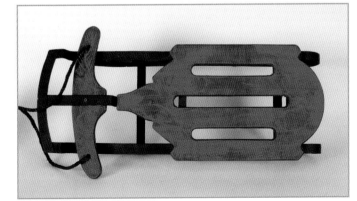

I found an old abandoned sled when I was in the ski town of Mammoth, California. I loved the memories that the sled brought back. I like to use sleds to decorate for Christmas. You may have an old family sled that is sitting in a dusty corner somewhere. You can find them at yard sales, thrift stores, or antique stores.

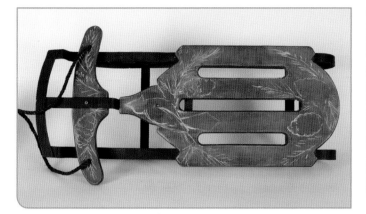

1.

Sand the sled if the wood needs to be smoothed. Remember to follow the wood grain.

Draw your pattern onto the sled with a white charcoal pencil, or trace it on with charcoal paper. The size of your sled will help you decide what design to use. I put a cardinal on the main part of the sled. That was the biggest section of the sled.

2.

Usually, most older sleds already have a brown color to them. Start by applying a color wash of red acrylic to the cardinal. Remember that a wash is made up of paint and a little water.

Apply the paint on with a flat brush. Put one coat of the red wash on the bird. You will have the color but be able to see the wood grain. This will also make the sled look antique.

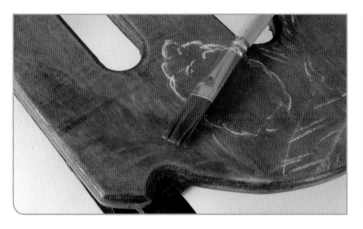

3.

Make a wash with Christmas green acrylic paint. Apply the paint onto the pine needles. Do a lighter wash (containing a little more water) on the bottom of the pine needles. Start at the center and pull the brush out, forming the needles. I am using a #10 flat brush.

4.

Make the wash a little brighter by using less water so you get more color. Turn your brush sideways and pull the brush out to form more pine needles. You are creating the background color which will really bring your design to life.

Paint all the pine needles on the sled. The pine needles should come out from the pine cones on the bottom part of the sled. Position the pine needles going up the wood pieces on the sled. The pine needles on the top of the sled should all be attached to a pine branch. Have pine needles come down the wood pieces at the top as well.

5.

Since the pine cones are already brown, do not paint them. Float a dark drown or burnt umber around the pine cones. If you need help, refer back to floating in Chapter 9. Floating brown around the pine cones will bring the pine cones forward so they do not fade into the background. The darkest part of the float should be along the outside of the pine cones.

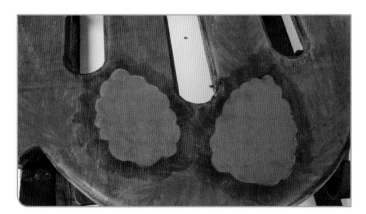

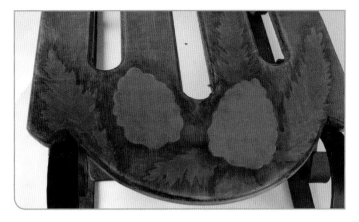

6.

Float around the pine needles, with the dark part going into the needles. If you have a very dark colored sled, you might want to try black paint.

7.

Float around the bird, pine cones, and pine needles on the top of the sled. You can go back over the floats again, once the first layer is dry, to darken them.

8.

Using a round brush with dark brown paint, draw on the tree branch. Start fatter on the left side and show more narrow branches on the right side. Make sure that branches connect to all of the pine needles and pine cones. The branch should be positioned so that the bird looks like he is sitting on the branch.

Add a little highlight to the branch with your round brush and a little straw color.

Base coat the bird's bill with straw yellow.

If you have a hole in the sled like this one shown, you could use QuikWood to fill it and sand it when it is dry.

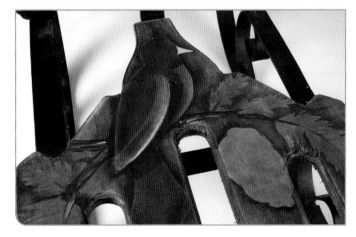

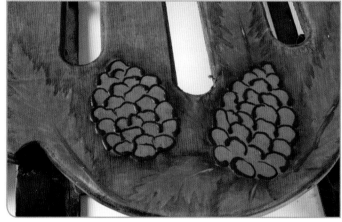

9.

Float white up the wing to create the top wing. Float white on the chest of the bird. If you are comfortable floating color you can also do a small float under the bird's bill to form the neck and head. Float with a darker red, like barn red. Float up against the top wing on the bottom tail and the very tip of the tail at the bottom.

10.

Once you have floated color on the design, start applying the wax. With brown wax and a smaller tool, create the pine cones one petal at a time. The petals are created with one or two curved strokes. Start the stroke on the outside of the pine cones and work toward the middle. You can mix up the strokes in the middle of the pine cones. Complete all of the pine cones.

11.

With the wax liner, add little lines in the top part of each pine cone petal. For wider petals, do two lines.

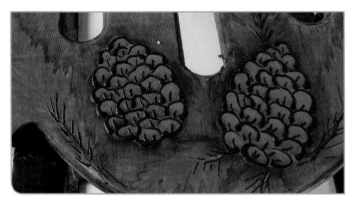

12.

Still using the wax liner, outline the branches and pull some brown lines into the beginning of the pine needles.

13.

With a small wax tool pull a dandelion stroke down the middle of the bill.

Pull a stroke on the bottom of the bill, coming to a sharp tail.

Pull a stroke on the top of the bill, meeting up with the other two strokes.

You can add feet to the cardinal if you like. Pull one stroke down from the body for the legs and have three small strokes meet to form the feet.

14.

Start at the top of the cardinal with a smaller wax tool; pull a red stroke from the top of the bill to the top of the bird's head. Pull a stroke on the other side to form his top feathers. Pull a very small stroke under the bill to form his neck. Pull a little tiny stroke from the neck to the bottom of the bill. Make a dot with your white charcoal pencil, so you know where the eye will go. Pull two smaller strokes, or more if needed, to fill in the head area.

Change to a larger tool; pull a stroke from the back section of the neck to the top knot. Moving to the wings, start a little in and just under the last stroke on the head. Pull the stroke curved out until you are on the outside of the wing.

Move down and pull the next stroke the same way, meeting up with the tail of the last stroke. Continue to pull the stroke until you run out of wax. Continue to work your way down the left side of the wing.

Leave enough room at the bottom for the right side stroke to come in. On the right side of the wing, start the stroke where you added the highlight. It should be close to meeting up with the top stroke on the left side. Curve the stroke to the right until it is on the edge of the wing.

Move down and pull the next stroke, meeting up with the tail of the last stroke. Continue all the way down the right side of the wing.

Pull a stroke from the middle of the bird's chest up to the neck. Pull a stroke starting at the beginning of the last stroke and pull it the opposite direction to form the chest. Pull a stroke at the beginning of the tail feathers to meet up with the last stroke. Pull one large stroke down the center of the chest to fill that area.

Start at the end of the tail feathers in the middle and pull a long stroke until you run out of wax. Pull a stroke on the right side of the tail feathers' edge; repeat on the left side. Fill in that area with as many strokes as you need. Pull a couple of strokes where the tail feather strokes end to the body of the bird to fill in that area.

Take a breath. The hard part is over. It is all fun from here.

Dot the eye with a black dot. You can add a little white reflective light to the eye with white acrylic paint.

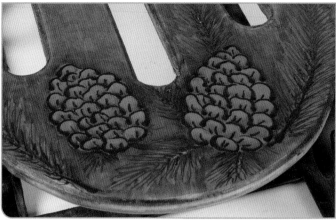

15.

With green wax, warm the MJ Wax liner and apply the pine needles. Start at the end of each pine needle section and add lots of needles a line at a time. It is okay to go over the brown lines that you put on earlier. Stop and warm your tool; then reload when the wax runs out or it gets cold. Do all of the pine needles.

16.

Add a few little bunches of needles coming out from under the pine cones. Make sure that you clean your wax tool out while it is warm and clean the inside with a Q-Tip.

17.

For highlight and texture, add yellow-green lines with the wax liner to the pine needles. This will help brighten up the design.

How do you want to varnish the sled? You should have a good idea of what you like or what would work best.

...Things to Think About...

- How about instead of a bird, put Christmas ornaments hanging down on each sled section?
- How about drawing a bow at the bottom, instead of pine cones, but still using the pine needles?
- How about drawing a snowman on the sled?
- You could create a design with snowflakes, making it blue, white, purple, and silver to make it more "wintery."
- What if you added a big Christmas ribbon to the sled?
- Sit the sled by the front door or fireplace with poinsettias. in fact, how about poinsettias on the sled?

Just think of the things you like
and come up with your own ideas.
There are Christmas patterns, bird patterns,
and snowflake patterns at
www.miriamjoy.com
to help you if you need help.

What says "fall" more than a harvest scene on a saw. Place it above the fireplace or sit it on the hearth. Place some small pumpkins around the saw to really give it that Thanksgiving flair.

A lot of artists like to paint on saws. This is another item that you can find in the family treasures, maybe in an old barn or house. If not, you can purchase one.

What sold me on this saw was the wood design it had. The carved wheat handle influenced the design I'd chosen. To me the saw screamed "harvest," so I let the piece tell me what it wanted to be.

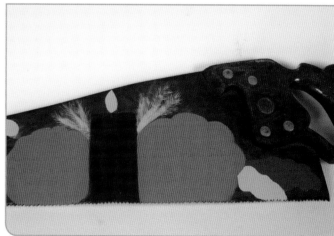

1.

Sand off any rust and clean the saw with rubbing alcohol to remove any grease.

I drew the pattern on with my white charcoal pencil. I started with the bigger designs like the candle and pumpkins placed in the bigger area of the saw. I filled in with leaves under the saw handle in the smaller area. Next, I drew gourds onto the saw, followed by corn which fit perfectly on the end of the saw. What do you think of when you think of "harvest"? You might have a different design in mind.

2.

Base coat the pumpkins with acrylic paint in pumpkin or orange, depending on the shade you want the pumpkins. I wanted a different look for the candle so I did a red wash to give it an older feel. The candle flame, one of the leaves, and the wheat were base coated in straw and the other leaf in red. On the wheat, pull lines out from the middle using a rake or fan brush.

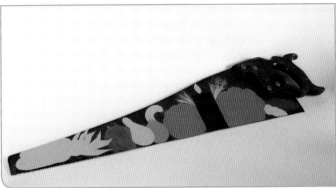

3.

Base coat the middle gourd and the top of the gourd to the right with straw-colored paint. The bottom of the gourd on the right is base coated in leaf green. The gourd to the left is painted with Christmas green. I left the gourd a little streaky. The corn was base coated with a tan color.

4.

You may have a bigger saw and may need to add some things to the design. You can always add more than one item, like the two pumpkins. If your saw is smaller, you may need to take out some of the items to make it fit the saw. Leaves are a good filler if needed.

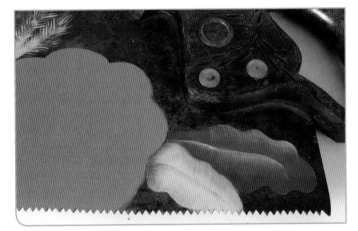

5.

I am going to refer the dark floats as "shading" and the lighter floats as "highlighting."

Starting with the straw leaf, shade under the pumpkin and down the bottom side of the leaf with a dark brown. Shade the vein in the middle of the leaf. Highlight the top of the leaf with orange. Shade the bottom of the red leaf with dark brown and purple. Highlight the top leaf and center vein with straw.

6.

Shade the back ear of corn with dark brown it to make it appear to be behind the other corn. Shade the bottom first corn and under the corn husk on the corn. Shade the top husk on the bottom or any that should be behind other husk.

Highlight with straw the opposite areas that you shaded, for example, the top of the corn and the top of the corn husk where you would have reflective light.

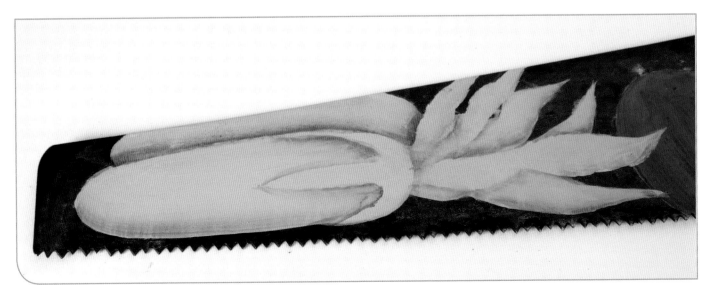

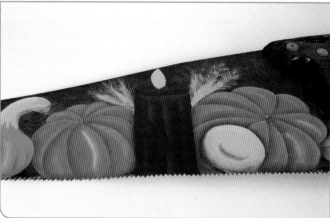

7.

Start with the gourd on the left. Start at the middle and shade to the right, behind each section to give it ridges, using forest green.

Shade where the gourd is under the yellow gourd. Start again at the middle and shade the ridges on the left. Make sure to take the shading around the top back as well. Highlight with white in the middle of the front areas to show reflective light. Float the white on the right and come back right next to that float going the opposite direction and float white so the white is solid in the middle and fades out on both sides. This is referred to as a center float.

On the yellow gourd, shade the bottom going out from the center to form the ridges with dark brown. Shade along the bottom of the gourd to create a shadow. Shade the ridges coming down from the top of the gourd. Highlight white on the right side of the gourd because it is in front. Do a center highlight, like you did in the last gourd, down the middle of the gourd to reflect light. Highlight the top of the gourd. Shade the green-yellow gourd under the top yellow gourd and around the bottom of the gourd with Christmas green. Starting at the center, shade to each side to create the sides. Add a center highlight down the center. Highlight the top neck of the gourd that would reflect light. Shade the bottom of the neck with dark brown. Shade dark brown to form the ridges of the neck.

8.

Starting at the middle of the pumpkins, shade the ridges of the pumpkin with red-orange to the right; come back and shade the ridges to your left. With yellow, highlight the opposite sides of the ridges. Add some center highlights to the front and wherever you feel it is needed. Go over a couple of the front highlights with white to make them stand out.

Shade around the small gourd on the pumpkin with dark brown. Shade the bottom of the gourd. Put a half circle shade in the center of the gourd. Highlight the top of the gourd with white.

Shade the candle with dark brown on both sides to give it a round shape. Drop down from the top of the candle, just a little, and shade a long, oval shape to create the top melted part of the candle. The flame should be in the middle of this section. Highlight some areas starting at the top of the candle coming down and some at the bottom going up to form the wax dripping.

9.

Spray varnish the saw blade at this time. I found that the metal was cold and the strokes did not want to pull. If the strokes still act cold, heat the saw blade with your embossing gun. You can heat it from the back as well. I heated each section as I worked on the saw. Make sure you do not heat any wax that you have on the design as it will melt. You could also place a heating pad on low under the saw as you work.

10.

Start warming up your melting pots and add your crayon to create the wax.

Start with the candle flame. At the bottom of the center of the flame, make a blue stroke up each side of the flame. Start next to the blue strokes and add a red stroke up each side of the candle. Next to the red strokes, pull an orange stroke up the sides. Pull a bigger dandelion stroke from the bottom of the orange to the top of the candle flame. Pull a small black stroke from the middle top of the candle into the candle flame. Heat the flame with your embossing tool until the wax is melted and it starts to run together. Do these steps before you put any other wax on the saw, so you do not melt the other wax.

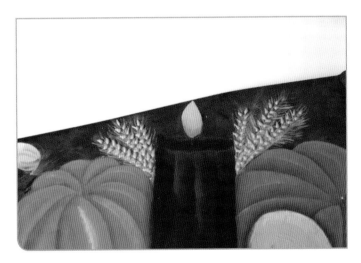

11.

With the MJ Wax Liner, put a line down the center of the wheat stalk. Create lines coming out from the middle of the wheat stalk. Start at the bottom and work your way up both sides. Have the lines come out farther than the paint background. Using a #0 tool for the small grains of wheat, start at the bottom and set the stroke down and pull it up like you did to create the fern leaves. Do wheat grains on both sides of the stalk and one on top.

12.

To form the stem of the pumpkin, go to the center of the pumpkin; pull brown strokes with a large tool, one at a time, next to each other. The wax should be warm and it will run together. Have the strokes end at different lengths on top. Pull orange strokes from the bottom of the pumpkin up. Pull strokes from the top down to meet the first strokes. You can put another stroke in the middle if you have room between the two strokes. Put dandelion strokes over the highlights. Pull the strokes from the top downward.

With red wax, create the drips on the candle. Start at the bottom and pull the strokes up. You can overlap the strokes. On the top left side of the candle, pull a long stroke in both directions to form the top. Repeat on the right top side. You can add strokes in between if the strokes do not meet up.

For the little gourd, divide the gourd into quarters; pull three strokes from the outside to the middle with orange wax. Repeat on the other side. Pull two strokes from each side of the gourd. Fill the rest of the gourd in with dandelion strokes.

13.

Starting at the bottom of the leaf and working your way toward the tip, pull orange strokes out following the outside of the yellow leaf. When the stroke ends, start a new stroke pulling it toward the tip. Do both sides of the leaf. Pull strokes down the middle of the leaf. Pull strokes out from the middle to create the veins. Repeat with red strokes on the red leaf.

14.

Starting with the Christmas green gourd, create the stem using brown wax, like you did with the pumpkin. Pull green strokes on top of the ridges, from the top downward. Pull strokes from the bottom of the gourd upward, meeting up with the first strokes.

For the yellow gourd and yellow-green gourd, add a little white to the brown and pull strokes to create the stems. Starting at the top of the yellow gourd, pull dandelion strokes downward where you shaded for the ridges. Pull a stroke on each side of the gourd where the last strokes ended. Moving to the bottom, pull a long stroke up each ridge. Pull a second set of strokes starting just up the tail and to the side of the last strokes you did.

Start at the top of the yellow-green gourd and pull strokes on top of the ridges you made. Pull long strokes down from that on each side, as many strokes as needed, until you reach the green part of the gourd. Add a couple strokes in the middle of the neck to fill in the area. Switch to yellow-green and pull long strokes up from the bottom. Leave some space and pull another set of strokes above the strokes you just made, having them reach the top part of the green gourd.

15.

Start at the top of the corn and pull long dandelion strokes down each side, one after another, until you reach the bottom. Pull strokes along the husk meeting at the tail. Make descending dots on the inside of the corn to create the kernels. Do the dots in dandelion, brown, and tan (made with brown and white). Alternate these colors and add strokes to the top husk starting on the outside of each piece and put a couple of strokes in the middle.

16.

Place your texture insert on an empty well and melt dandelion crayon on top. Pounce into the wax with the Texture Brush. Pounce dandelion on the top husk to create the silk of the corn. Pounce a little on the very ends of the corn. This also helps to fill in the area.

Think about how you want to varnish or seal the saw. Do you need it heatproof? If you wanted a yellow look to make it look older, you could use marine varnish.

...Things to Think About...

Remember: The wax adds a whole new dimension. Paint is just flat and the wax added a puffiness or 3D look to the project. Even pictures do not do the project justice because you are still looking at a flat picture.

- What if you did the saw with jack-o'-lanterns and leaves for Halloween?
- For Christmas you could make poinsettias and Christmas bulbs.
- You might like a design that you can keep out year-round.
- How about putting a man's name onto the saw with masculine colors and some circle designs for a garage or tool room?
- What about a fish jumping out of the water with a fish hook glued on?

Conclusion

In this holiday book, I wanted to really challenge you: starting with simple projects and ending up with advanced projects and teaching you wax designs that work great for the different holidays. I wanted to show you how to make wonderful ornaments or jewelry with the twice-melted wax and for you to see how easy it is to make a wonderful gift or decoration for any occasion. It was important that I make you think about everyday items that you can turn into a work of art for each holiday season—taking the ordinary and turning it into the extraordinary, pushing you a little with color-based projects to change the whole look of the wax design. I hope you have as much fun as I do with the holidays and wax!

Should you need to contact me, please email me at **Art@miriamjoy.com**. I make every effort to return your email within twenty-four hours of receiving it.

I can be reached through the social media websites listed below:

Facebook: **Miriam Joy's Waxy Crafty Corner**
Facebook: **Miriam Joy Gourd Creations**
Pinterest: **www.pinterest.com/miriamjoysagen**
YouTube: **www.youtube.com/user/Miriamjoy123**

Thank you for purchasing this book and supporting my artistic ideas and products.

God bless,
Miriam Joy

Miriam Joy's Products and Supplies

I invite you take time visit the MJ products that I have featured in this book. I am constantly updating this page with new and innovative products for you to enjoy. The website with featured products can be found at **www.miriamjoy.com.**

I am constantly working on new projects and new YouTube videos for you. You can subscribe to my YouTube channel so that you can get all the latest videos on YouTube at Miriamjoy123 or type in the direct link **https://www.youtube.com/user/Miriamjoy123.**

I also have a Facebook page at "Miriam Joy's Waxy Crafty Corner." I post pictures of projects and other craft items on this page for you to make and be inspired.

For your convenience I offer Paypal or any major credit card should you wish to purchase products from my website.